WHAT PEOPLE ARE SAYING ABOUT
The Art of Making Decisions
Expanding Common Sense & Experience

Dr. Wirasinghe's book, *The Art of Making Decisions,* can help managers lead their staff through the maze of daily decisions found in any small or large business.

— Dr. Doug Elliot
Bechtel Fellow; Fellow of the AICHE
President and COO—IPSI LLC, A Bechtel Affiliated Company

Decision-making is an essential life-skill. This is a refreshingly new treatment of a complex subject. I found it very informative.

— Dr. Michelle Michot Foss
Executive Director
Institute for Energy, Law & Enterprise, University of Houston

With simplicity, common sense, and eloquence, Dr. Wirasinghe has presented in his book an irrefutable case for a sound decision-making technique.

— Edward A. Monto
Director, MetroBank, N.A.
Chairman, Ex-Im Bank's 2002 Advisory Committee

Often we make even complex decisions without much thinking, and repent later when they turn out to be wrong. This book handles the complex subject of decision-making in a lucid manner. I found the book very easy reading. Errol has succeeded to a great extent in making the process of decision-making into a science, and that too in a simple way.

— Dr. Bhamy V. Shenoy
International Oil Expert
Former Manager Strategic Planning, Conoco

Decision-making is an essential life-skill. *The Art of Making Decisions* truly helps a person to expand common sense and experience. It is easy to read, and the subject is well presented. This is a book every young professional should read.

— DR. RAUL MONTEFORTE
Commissioner, Energy Regulatory Commission of Mexico

———

Dr. Wirasinghe's book, *The Art of Making Decisions*, is a refreshingly new approach to decision-making. The seven-step method is an excellent road map for a thought process that will result in the best decision possible with the information available.

— FELIX SPIZALE
General Manager—Texaco International Pipeline LLC

———

Dr. Wirasinghe's straightforward analysis, based on his many years of hands-on experience, has produced a valuable book on decision-making. This book provides invaluable information for students and professionals alike.

— DR. GARVIN WATTUHEWA
Physics Professor—Alabama School of Mathematics and Science

———

With the ever-increasing flood of data bombarding us, the need to sort out the chaff from valuable information becomes more critical every day. Dr. Wirasinghe's techniques are particularly helpful in this regard.

—DR. HARRY H. WEST
P.E.; CSP

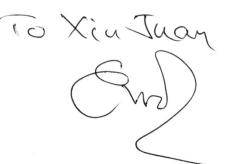

To Xiu Juan

THE ART OF
Making
Decisions

Expanding Common Sense & Experience

Errol Wirasinghe, PhD

SHANMAR
PUBLISHING
Houston

Inquiries should be sent to:
Shanmar Publishing
13722 Camelot Centre Ct.
Houston, TX 77069, USA

E-mail: author@XpertUS.com
Website: www.XpertUS.com

Copy Editing and Final Proofing: Shirin Wright: proofwrite@hotmail.com

Structural Editing: Gary Twitchell: ether1@ix.netcom.com

Cover Photography by: Picturequest: Brand X Pictures, Steve Allen, Photographer

Cover Design, Book Composition, and Print Coordination: Argent Associates, Boulder, Colorado: argentcorp@aol.com

1. SELF-HELP / Personal Growth / General
2. BUSINESS & ECONOMICS / Decision-Making & Problem-Solving
3. EDUCATION / Decision-Making & Problem-Solving

Library of Congress Control Number: 2002112762

Wirasinghe, Errol
    The Art of Making Decisions: Expanding Common Sense & Experience
    Includes index.

ISBN: 0-9722387-0-0 (Pbk)

First published in 2003

Printed in the United States of America

A Note to the Reader

Disclaimer

The tools and techniques discussed in this book are guidelines for effective decision-making. Neither the author nor the publisher offers guarantees of any sort, either direct or implied.

The *XpertUS* decision-maker does not make decisions for you. You make the decision. *XpertUS* is a method that guides you to a balanced decision.

Readers who opt to use the proposed tools and techniques do so entirely at their own risk. The final outcome depends on the user's judgment.

Acknowledgments

—⟨⟩—

My sincere thanks to my dear friend, Gary Twitchell, who spent many hours reviewing the original material and offering suggestions. Along with his wife, Kim Twitchell, he was a tremendous source of inspiration to me in this writing endeavor.

Thanks also to many friends who provided valuable insight:
Ruth Narendran; Ed Monto; Saroja Gunaratne; Chaethana Yalamanchili; Dudley Anderson.

A special thanks to Kurt Lieber for his many suggestions.

I take this opportunity to extend a special thank you to Shirin Wright, my editor and proofreader, for her tireless efforts at making this book as error-free as possible.

Coordination of the production of this book was in the experienced hands of Alan Bernhard of Argent Associates, who ensured that quality was never compromised. Thank you, Alan, for your dedicated efforts.

Dedication

—◁◁⌇▷▷—

To my loving wife and partner in life, Aruni,
Who had to endure many lonely nights and weekends
while I was glued to the computer.

Who took care of all the mundane work, while
I was focused 100% on the task at hand.

Whose insight helped enormously to improve
the readability of this book.

Her love and patience were my strength and comfort.
Without her sacrifices
this book would never have been written.

—◁◁⌇▷▷—

To our children, Rushani and Marco,
who continued to encourage me
during my moments of despair.

Contents

Preface   xi

Part I – Fundamentals   *1*

1. Introduction   *3*
2. Bad Decisions and the Experts   *13*
3. Types of Decisions   *21*
4. Tools and Techniques   *31*
5. Inherent Limitations   *43*
6. External Factors Beyond Our Control   *59*
7. Thinking Creatively   *75*
8. Time—Invaluable and Perishable   *95*
9. Selecting Criteria and Candidates   *99*
10. The Ranking Process   *109*
11. *XpertUS* and the Pairwise Technique   *121*
12. Implementing Your Decision   *127*
13. Working With Others   *133*
14. Collaborative Negotiations   *141*

Part II – The 7-Step Guide To Bulletproof Your Decisions   *149*

Part III – Applications and Case Studies   *159*

1. Purchasing—Bid Evaluation   *163*
2. Human Resources   *169*

3. Personal—Selecting a Partner/Spouse *179*
4. Real Estate—Buying a Home *183*
5. Buying an Automobile *187*
6. Career Guidance—Which Profession? *189*
7. Career Guidance—Which University? *191*
8. Selecting a School *193*
9. Deciding On a Small Business *195*
10. Small Business Advertising Campaign *199*

PART IV – APPENDICES (For Further Reading) *201*

1. Selecting a Good Decision-Making Tool *203*
2. Case Study: Downing of Libyan Airliner *207*
3. Brainstorming *211*
4. *XpertUS*—Virtues and Reliability *217*
5. The Proposal *223*
6. A Guide to Negotiating *225*
7. Job Categories—U.S. Department of Labor *229*
8. Test Your Decision-Making Prowess—Some Examples *231*
9. Answers to Problems *239*

References *243*

Index *245*

The "Aim-Preset"™ Technique *251*

Gift Certificate *253*

Author Biography *255*

Preface

A CEO may have to decide if he/she should compete against a rival, or acquire the rival. A mother may have to decide if she should send her son to a state college, or borrow money to send him to a more expensive private university. To the people involved, these are crucial decisions.

Depending on the circumstances, people make decisions in a host of ways, including dictatorial/monarchical declarations, egotistical assertions, praying to higher powers, seeking advice from fortune-tellers, delegating to subordinates, passing the buck to colleagues, postponement, common sense, past experience, gambling, relying on committees, following established rules or traditions, superstition, and mathematical analysis.

In 1956, the famous American psychologist Dr. George Miller[1] wrote a paper entitled, *The Magic Number Seven, Plus or Minus Two,* in which he said: "The conscious mind can hold seven, plus or minus two, pieces of information at a time, either from internal thought or from the external world." Yet, most of us never acknowledge such human limitations.

I am certain many of you are convinced that, when it comes to decision-making, you can do as good a job as the next person. Therefore, I present a few glaring examples of questionable decisions.

In recent years, some decisions made by U.S. presidents have come back to haunt us:

- When given the opportunity to apprehend Osama bin Laden, President Bill Clinton opted not to authorize his capture. Today, Osama bin Laden and his Al-Qaeda are threatening the peaceful existence of Western civilization. Bin Laden has become the most wanted man in the world, with millions of dollars earmarked for his capture.

- President George Bush (Sr.) had the opportunity and the means to remove Saddam Hussein from the Iraqi leadership, yet stopped short of capturing him. Finally the U.S. government had to pay a very high price, in both human and monetary terms, to depose Saddam.

There are differing views as to whether these presidents made optimum decisions; the debate will continue for years to come.

Talented executives from very successful companies have made radically different decisions with the same information and in the same time frame.

- When Ford Motor Company rejected Harold Sperlich's idea of the *minivan*, they probably lost out on one of the greatest opportunities in the history of the auto industry. Sperlich teamed up with Lee Iacocca at Chrysler, who took up the challenge; today 50% of all household vehicles are either minivans or SUVs.

- When IBM turned down the offer, the Rank Organization bought the rights to develop Xerox's copier process outside the U.S. Today, revenues from this venture alone are sufficient to support the entire Rank Organization.

One does not need to look far to see authoritative claims by experts that have turned out to be totally inaccurate. Here are a few examples:

- "This bomb will never go off. I speak as an expert in explosives" (Admiral William Leahy of the U.S. Atomic Bomb Project, 1940).

- "I recommend that the U.S. Patent Office be shut down, since everything that could be invented has already been invented" (Charles Duell, Director of the U.S. Patent Office, 1899).

Decision-making is not problem solving. Problem solving is unique to each *problem*. Decision-making is unique to the *decision-maker*.

As an example, imagine that you and your spouse are planning the purchase of a new home. Both of you would identify your criteria, and then work with an agent to find some houses. After a few visits, you would select four or five houses that meet your specifications. At this point you have solved your *problem*. Now, you might have a preference toward one house, while your spouse might decide on a different house—because the *decision* is unique to each of you.

Recently I met an entomologist, who was tackling the problem of worms attacking grape vines in the Napa Valley. He had identified six possible methods of treatment, each of which had advantages and disadvantages, and was struggling with the final decision. This is a good example of an expert with domain-specific knowledge, identifying available solutions. The expert had solved the *problem*. Subsequently, a management team used the *XpertUS* decision-maker software to make the final *decision*.

Decision-making is inherently complicated because of a multitude of factors (see box). Many of these factors were at play in the (erroneous) downing of a Libyan Airliner by Israeli Defense Forces in 1973 (Appendix 2).

There are a host of tools and techniques available for decision-making, ranging from operational research techniques to probability theories to root-cause analysis methods. These are limited because of their inability to handle subjective input. Additionally, these techniques are beyond the skill and/or finances of most people, including most managers. Let us not forget that the study of decision-making is the study of human judgment.

When faced with a decision-making scenario, the mind goes through two steps:

1. Instantaneously identifies all available options (creative thinking).

2. Decides on the most appropriate one (decision-making).

Factors at Play!

1. Poorly defined objective
2. Uncertainties of information
3. Global objectives and goals
4. Context and Environment
5. Multiple decision-makers
6. High stakes
7. Time pressure

The role of creativity is that of generating and identifying options with which to solve a problem. The role of decision-making is that of ranking these options. Decision-making is universal: Negotiations, Vendor Selection, Planning, Recruiting, Team Selection, Bid Evaluations, Parenting, Coaching, to name a few areas, all involve decision-making.

In 1941, creative thinking helped the British army defeat Hitler on many fronts. Montgomery's "Desert Fox" enlisted Jasper Maskelyne, a famous magician, to deceive the Germans. Maskelyne and his Magic Gang of 14 (specialists in analytical chemistry, electrical engineering, and stage-set construction) were involved in an elaborate operation to set up a fake harbor in a nearby bay. This involved constructing dummy buildings, a dummy lighthouse and even dummy anti-aircraft batteries which fired thunderflashes. The ploy was successful, as it diverted German bombers from the port of Alexandria. This is a notable example of how *creative thinking* played a decisive role in changing the history of the world!*

* The British government has sealed other tricks Maskelyne used during WWII, for 100 years. These will be released in the year 2049.

Even the best decision-making tool or technique will be of little value unless you have creatively identified viable options. Thus creative thinking is an integral part of good decision-making. By the same token, there are many who are capable of identifying very creative solutions, but are incapable of making a decision.

On August 4, 2003, 12-year-old Sho Yano became the youngest student ever to enter the University of Chicago's Medical School. Sho Yano was gifted with above-average intelligence, but had no experience. We adults have experience! *Thinking* is the process that links our *intelligence* to our *experience*. We need to develop and hone our thinking skills.

Regardless of all my preaching, there will be some who think there is no substitute for common sense and experience. Others will continue to insist that they can write down a few criteria, review all pros and cons, and make an optimum decision.

Mahatma Gandhi, Nelson Mandela, Martin Luther King, Jr., and Abraham Lincoln were all talented leaders—their ideas were revolutionary and unorthodox. They made courageous decisions and then executed them with steadfast conviction and tenacious persistence. They brought about changes that were unthinkable to the average mind. How do we make such superior decision-making prowess available to everyone?

Most books on the subject of decision-making do not meet the needs of the average person. They are either mathematical or psychological, and directed at academia, or research establishments. That is not to say that mathematics has no place in decision-making. For example, the insurance industry uses statistical techniques and probability theories to determine pricing. Statistical analysis, forecasting techniques, and operational research techniques are extremely useful tools; but in the end, most decisions are based on individual human perception, values, emotions, and circumstances. This book is not a complicated treatise on mathematics or philosophy; it is a practical guide to decision-making presented in lay terms.

You have been trained to walk, to talk, to write, to play . . . and, in your profession. Naturally you are very good at these activities. Yet, you have not been trained to make decisions—something you do every day. How can you expect to make optimum decisions, when you have not had any training in this area?

This book is aimed at everyone: high school students, homemakers, managers, CEOs, school board administrators, senators, congressmen, and presidents. It provides the tools and techniques required to make optimum decisions. It carries a special message for those who survive on mantras such as: "If it ain't broke, don't fix it" or, "not on my watch."

Do not hide behind traditions! Traditions are simply innovations that were successful.

I have included examples from diverse cultures and industries to convince the reader that decision-making problems have no boundaries. Success in any endeavor depends on the vision and the passion of individuals.

The first few chapters present the fundamental elements of decision-making. Some readers might find this somewhat boring. I encourage you to be patient, and read through these sections. In the subsequent chapters you will learn new techniques to enhance your decision-making skills.

Part One

Fundamentals

The quality of your decision will depend on:

1. Data & Information (problem domain)
2. Context Information
3. Creative Options
4. Solution Technique Used
5. Expertise (of the decision-maker)

However, the final outcome will depend on:

a. Appropriate Timing
b. Adequate Resources
c. Commitment to Execution!

One

Introduction

"When dealing with people ......
you are not dealing with creatures of logic,
but creatures of emotions."
— DALE CARNEGIE

In the early 1990s Smith-Corona and Brother were vying for the top spot in the typewriter business. Smith-Corona was the undisputed leader (since 1886); but the Japanese company, Brother, was rapidly encroaching on their territory. Smith-Corona thought the problem was production costs, which were high in the U.S. as compared to the lower costs in Asia. Based on this perception, they moved their production operations to Mexico.* Brother did exactly the opposite — they moved their operations from Japan to the United States. Same problem, same time frame — totally different decisions, totally different outcomes!

Recently, Peter Drucker, the renowned management guru, said that President George W. Bush's decision to impose tariffs on steel imports was a mistake. Same information, same time frame — different conclusions.** Forget the outcome. What is important is that they disagreed on a technical issue! Were their objectives the same? How do we know whose decision is the correct one or the better one?

---

* In 1995, Smith-Corona finally filed for bankruptcy protection.
** Twenty months later President Bush reversed his decision.

The Human Element

What is clear is that we need to be *objective* in our decision-making. Being *objective* is to remove excessive personal bias and preferences from the decision-making process. When we fail to be *objective*, we are being *subjective*. We let our values, emotions, experiences, and ego excessively bias decisions, which prevents us from reaching the optimum decision.

Subjectivity

A recent study on grading of essays showed that 50% of the professors gave a different grade to the same essay; on a scale of 1-5, some were two grades apart. The study also showed that male lecturers tend to place greater importance on argument, while female lecturers are more concerned with the amount of effort a student makes. It concluded that getting a good grade was like winning the lottery.

—The Institute for Policy Studies in Education at the University of London

Subjectivity may occur by omission or it may be intentional. Subjectivity by omission translates into ignorance, negligence, or incompetence, while intentional subjectivity represents arrogance, corruption, nepotism, cravings, aversions, ego, and the like. Both can lead to undesirable, even catastrophic, consequences. True, as long as humans make decisions, subjectivity will be present; but we must strive to minimize its influence on our decisions, especially when such decisions have an impact on others.

Many studies document that a majority of decisions is highly subjective (see box). Often, the typical manager, CEO, or head of the household makes a decision based on a hunch or an educated guess—and then legitimizes that decision with pseudo-rational arguments. Volumes have been written on bad decisions made in the corporate sector. I have presented some interesting examples in Chapter 2.

In an attempt to minimize subjectivity, many decision-makers have turned to quantitative (measurable) data. Unfortunately, people do not realize that even pure numbers are interpreted by subjective people and may even have been derived from subjective sources. All decisions are driven by *qualitative* interpretations of *quantitative* data.

If asked to decide between two travel guides—where there is a 50% probability that Jack has a "lot of knowledge of the terrain", and a 50% probability that David has "no knowledge of the terrain", most would opt for Jack. Many researchers have confirmed this type of human tendency. Yet, in reality, both have the same level of knowledge.

For example, a room temperature of 75° may or may not be pleasant, depending on your personal preference. Here quantitative information has a qualitative value. If cost and comfort are two of the criteria, one person might decide to pay more for central air, while another might decide to buy a fan, and someone else might decide to do nothing and endure some discomfort. This subjectivity is a reflection of preferences, resources, theories, state of mind, etc.

The US economy owes its existence to *subjectivity!* One person might consider a share priced at $13.25 to be a great buy, while another will consider it to be a sell signal. If not for this subjective behavior, we would not have a stock market.

There are five principal traits that affect our ability to make decisions: *memory, experience, reasoning, comprehension (language)* and *knowledge.* Memory is important only in our ability to recall what we know of the other four.

A Troublesome Situation...

When making decisions, 88% of management admits to using gut-feelings over hard facts up to 75% of the time; 91% admit that they do not get enough thinking time, and 62% say that they do not get the right amount of information to make a decision.

Decision Making Survey, 1997
(Business Objects)

Is everyone equally competent in these five areas? Of course not! We are all unique; we have different levels of competence in each area. If our levels of expertise are different, when given the same set of options and information, we are likely to arrive at different decisions. These and other traits will be discussed throughout this book.

Imagine a situation where three people are planning to climb a mountain in the Himalayan foothills, where *safety* is not negotiable. One reads (*language*) about the dangers of the various routes; another has actually climbed similar mountains (*experience*); and the third communicates with the local folk, asking questions about the mountains and developing a sense of the environment (*knowledge*). Each has different levels of expertise in relation to *reasoning*. It is very likely that each one will select a different route up the mountain. Is anyone wrong? Probably not! Yet, one route will be the safest. How do we know which one?

As another example of such uniqueness, consider an artist, a lumberjack, and a botanist walking through a forest. Now, ask them to list ten items they observed. Each will have perceived and observed different things.

Change

What triggers the need for decisions is *change*. Sometimes change simply happens; sometimes we initiate change. When change happens, it creates problems, which demand solutions. As change evolves, one's success or failure depends on how one handles the impact of this change, and on how one reaches a balanced decision considering all the factors at play.

A good example of a well-orchestrated change is what happened in the automobile industry. While European manufacturers such as Mercedes Benz and Volvo were proudly maintaining their original designs, the Japanese changed their designs every couple of years to excite the public and to entice them to trade in their older vehicles for new ones. The Europeans did not react to this until the Japanese started increasing their market share with their newer and more attractive designs, creature comforts and colors.

Charles Darwin emphasized the importance of being responsive to change when he stated:

> *"It is not the strongest of the species that survive, nor the most intelligent, but the one most responsive to change."*

Balance and Comfort

Try telling someone that you would like to help him/her make a decision and you will probably be frowned upon. This is because everyone has a sense of pride in his/her ability to make good decisions. All decisions boil down to personal choices, which are usually based on *values, emotions, experience, circumstances,* etc. In the end, it is your decision and it needs to reflect your desires and values, otherwise you will not be successful at implementing it. However, there needs to be a balance; we are looking for the *yin-yang* of decision-making.

Several recent American presidents have struggled to find that balance when deciding whether to permit exploration for oil and gas in environmentally sensitive areas. They have to choose between preservation of the environment and our insatiable thirst for energy.

Making a decision is like weaving a tapestry. A tapestry is a combination of design, color, and weave, all of which involve personal choices that reflect the values, emotions, and resources of the designer. The final tapestry is a blend of many decisions. Indeed, like weaving a tapestry, decision-making is an art—the art of selecting the best from the many available factors and options.

Consider the controversial subject of the death penalty. Different nations have made different decisions not only on what crimes and circumstances merit the penalty of death, but also on the merit of the death penalty itself. Why have different countries reached different conclusions? It comes down to a balance among such factors as values, emotions, experience, and resources.

Although the U.S. Constitution is designed to allow government by the people, the structure clearly utilizes consensus in decision-making. It is no accident that the Senate and the House of Representatives provide the checks and balances needed for decisions of national importance. Mechanisms were set in place to help control subjectivity, and to provide transparency. However, as I will illustrate later, there are inherent perils associated with group decision-making as well.

Transparency

Transparency, an important requirement of today's decision-making, is defined as *the clarity of a process that conforms to established auditing principles.* For ease of demonstration, consider the tendering of large public projects. Government agencies are cognizant of political pressure, bribery, corruption, and nepotism. The organization responsible for this activity has to ensure that the selection process is *transparent* and *objective.* Yet, vested interest groups try to influence the final decision, usually through highly subtle means. Further, if a decision is not transparent, non-winning candidates or special-interest groups may question it, or even initiate legal proceedings.

Indeed, even if the selection process is honest and subject to strict monitoring, proving *objectivity* to the public and to governing authorities can be a daunting task.

The Information Technology (IT) Revolution

Think back to the days when your grandfather (or your great-grandfather) was trying to decide on a college. Was he faced with a difficult decision? It is highly probable he was in a small town, where there was only one college.

Now, consider a teenager in today's world. With so much information at hand and so many options, he/she has to consider a host of criteria (see box).

We can safely state that the more information and the more choices one has, the more difficult decision-making is. This will become abundantly clear as you progress through this book.

The Information Technology (IT) revolution and Enterprise Resource Planning (ERP) are the catalysts driving the corporate world today. IT and ERP are a result of the explosive growth of computers and Internet capabilities. Computers will get faster and technology will become better and more easily accessible to more people. Companies spend millions of dollars on IT and ERP implementation with the objective of providing management with more and better information, all in the hope of ending up with better decisions.

Selecting a College

- Distance from Home
- City or Small Town
- Primary Subject
- Cost of Tuition
- Cost of Living
- Scholarships
- Name Recognition
- Duration of Course
- Teacher to Student Ratio
- Academic Demands, etc.

But what is IT? IT encompasses gathering, organizing, and disseminating information.

Today's manager receives real-time data on manpower, sales, budgets, cash flow, financing, inventory, supplies, transport and distribution, share prices, market saturation, future pricing, currency fluctuations, geopolitical and regulatory issues, and more. He/she is faced with multi-dimensional problems and is forced to integrate mountains of information into the decision-making process. Yet, there has not been a substantial improvement in the decision-making process itself, and managers are saddled with slow, cumbersome and outdated decision-making tools—someone forgot to train the *decision-maker!*

When it comes to decision-making, *common sense and experience* are vital tools; however, they alone are not enough. As this book will show, emotions have their place, but they need to be held in check during decision-making. Occasionally, we do conduct decision analyses, but even then, we interpret the basic information based on our values and experience; gut-feelings are themselves a function of *common sense and experience.*

Today's management needs new training and new tools to make better decisions, while maintaining control of the process. No matter how skilled you are at decision-making, would it not be beneficial to check out an important decision using an advanced decision-making tool? Would it not give you an additional degree of confidence and some insurance? Even if you hire a consultant, he/she can only advise. *You* must make the final decision.

Problem Solving & Opportunity Seeking

In problem solving, we often know the *desired state*. This is what is referred to as a *close-ended* problem. Problem solving is only applicable to *close-ended* problems, where the desired state is known. *Open-ended* problems require *opportunity-seeking* techniques.

Most executives are good at solving problems. Often, those who get to the top of the management ladder are problem-solvers and troubleshooters. However, to most executives, an *opportunity* is a high-risk speculation, because it is in the future. Yet, *problem solving* without *opportunity seeking* would certainly lead to stagnation, and even extinction.

A friend of mine had an exclusive license to market carbonated drinks to elementary schools in the Houston area. But in August 2003, his business collapsed because the state passed a law banning carbonated drinks in these schools. It pays to try to anticipate future trends, and to innovate (seek new opportunities) continuously.

The *BiC* Corporation moved from ballpoint pens, to lighters, and then to disposable razors, continuously seeking new opportunities. The turtle can make progress only when it puts out its head; yet that is when it is most vulnerable. Likewise, the willingness to take risks is a prerequisite for opportunity seeking.

Everyone is surrounded by opportunities. But they will be seen only if they are sought! With a *problem* you search for the *solution*; with an *opportunity* you search for the *benefit*.

A problem is something you want to do, but cannot. An opportunity is something you do not know much about, but something you should be doing. Problem solving is *urgent*. Identifying opportunities is *important*!

Most of us have heard the phrase, *Not on my watch*. This is the greatest impediment to opportunity seeking. Sadly, executives who excel at *problem solving* subscribe to this thinking and consequently are reluctant to engage in *opportunity seeking*. Their philosophy is, *if it ain't broke, don't fix it*.

In the recruiting world, when a résumé is received, the *problem-solver* type will look at the list of openings, and say: "No, we do not have a vacancy that fits this person." The *opportunity-seeker* will recognize that the applicant has an unusual combination of talents, that are of potential value to the organization, and try to create a position to utilize these talents.

While the rest of the world was trying to miniaturize the cell phone, Japan's NTT DoCoMo company came up with the "Finger Whisper Phone", which operates on "bone conduction technology". The user wears a strap and places a finger in the ear to communicate. Activating and dialing is done by tapping the fingers.

While the manufacturers of the VCR were trying desperately to provide instantaneous locating and playback features, others were moving ahead with the DVD.

While telephone companies and cable operators were paying large sums of money to get access to lay their cables, satellite technology was making huge strides.

Recently, Google announced a massive free e-mail service, with several new features, to challenge the dominance of Yahoo and Hotmail, just when these two companies thought they had a monopoly in this area.

These are real examples of opportunity seeking. Those who do not venture into the unknown will suffer serious consequences, which could even mean extinction.

President Theodore Roosevelt was humble enough to admit that he often made bad decisions. How often have we admitted to having made a bad decision? If you are to benefit from reading this book, you must be willing to admit that you too are fallible.

If you have an insurmountable ego and believe that you are infallible, then there is nothing anyone can do to help you. But I would like to remind you of what former U.S. Secretary of State Henry Kissinger once said:

> *"Each success only buys you an admission ticket to a more difficult problem."*

For those of us who are somewhat more humble, this book may serve as a valuable source of reference. Even if the techniques I propose seem hard at first, the *XpertUS* software will allow you to use them with ease.

"If I could be right 75% of the time, it would be a high point in my life; in fact, anyone who can be right 55% of the time can go to Wall Street and become a millionaire."

— President T. Roosevelt

The purpose of any decision-making tool or technique is to assist the user in *ranking* available options. Therefore, in this book, when I refer to decision-making, I am providing the user with the means of prioritizing available options or choices.

Two

Bad Decisions and the Experts

"When you are green, you are growing; when you are ripe, you are rotting."

— Ray Kroc
Founder of McDonalds

It is easy to say that someone made a bad decision, but is there really such a thing as a bad decision? The answer is an emphatic *yes*. In fact, if documented, citations of bad decisions would surpass the *Oxford Dictionary* in volume. What constitutes a bad decision?

A decision is said to be "flawed" when it deviates from "classical" theory. However, any notion that the theory might be flawed is not entertained. It is only when an error is systematic that experts tend to modify the model. Otherwise they never challenge the model.

Often we classify a decision as good or bad depending on the outcome; this is the conventional view. At some time in the future a decision may appear as an error, often due to new information, but that does not make the original decision bad.

John Restivo, John Kogut, and Dennis Halstead were serving life sentences for the rape and murder of a teenage girl. On June

5, 2003, they were released (after 18 years), having been found innocent of the crime, based on DNA evidence. Was the original conviction a bad decision? Of course not!

Imagine you are trying to pick the winning horse in a race where the list of horses (candidates) is provided. You are given information about the event, distance, rider, and the horses (heritage, track record, etc.), but not about ground condition. Because of the ground condition, the horse you picked did not win. Yet this information was neither available to you nor considered. Another person who had this vital piece of information did pick the winner. Regardless of the outcome, you probably made the best possible decision based on the information you had. However, you probably could have improved your decision by using a more sophisticated tool or technique.

Now let us consider another example—the toss of a coin. I offer you $1,000 if it turns up heads, but for tails, you agree to give me $500. Ignoring any moral issues associated with gambling, would you play? Probably most of you would.

I flip the coin. Now I ask you, "*Without knowing the outcome of the first toss, would you play a second time under the same terms?*" Only some would agree to play.

I flip the coin a second time. Once again I ask you, "*Without knowing the outcome of either of the previous tosses, would you play a third time under the same terms?*"

When I asked this of nearly 100 people, almost 30% said they would not play a second time. Of those who agreed to play a second time, 80% said they would not play a third time. In other words, a total of 86% of all participants, including some senior executives, did not recognize the statistical advantage of continuing.

Simple laws of probability, however, indicate that your chances of winning are greatly enhanced as the number of plays increases. If your original decision was based on a sound analysis of the probability of success, you should play not just a second time, but as many times as it is offered to you. Though the probability of heads or tails on any individual flip is 50%, the amount you would win is double the amount you would lose; thus the more times you play, the more money you would win.

Hence, we may conclude that if a decision is based on a sound analysis, it remains a good decision, regardless of the outcome.

Bad Decisions?

One needs data to draw conclusions; however, having information or being learned about a subject does not necessarily make one a good decision-maker. Unfortunately, well-informed experts all over the world are making poor decisions. No wonder we have so many messy situations worldwide! Here are a few examples of bad decisions that have been studied and concluded to have been bad.

— Xerox

In 1979, the Xerox PARC group did not look favorably on their engineering group's *Mouse* and GUI (Graphical User Interface) ideas for a computer. Soon afterward, the Lisa and Macintosh computers (based on GUI) were developed and released by Apple. Today, the GUI principle is the *de facto* standard for computers.

— IBM

In 1980, IBM asked Microsoft to produce the operating system for its first personal computer. Microsoft purchased the QDOS operating system, renamed it MS-DOS, and then sold it to IBM for a substantial profit. IBM did not buy the license from Microsoft (bad decision), allowing Microsoft to freely sell this operating system to IBM's competitors. Today, Microsoft is worth billions of dollars.

— POINTCAST

Remember the streaming news from the Internet? Chris Hassett (of PointCast fame) was the inventor of this concept. It was reported that in 1997 News Corp was considering acquiring PointCast for about $400 million. The deal was never consummated. In 1999, Idealab acquired PointCast for about $10 million. Did Hassett miss a golden opportunity? What about News Corp—was their offer a bad decision?

— COCA-COLA

During its early days, Pepsi owners ran into financial difficulties and offered the company to Coca-Cola. Coke's management rejected the offer, saying there was no value in the Pepsi enterprise. Coke lost the once-in-a-lifetime opportunity to close down Pepsi. Today, Pepsi is a worthy rival to Coke.

— SONY BETA

Ask anyone in the recording industry and they will tell you the Betamax (Sony) format was far superior to the VHS format. JVC launched the VHS format eighteen months after Betamax came out. Yet, because of their liberal licensing policies, they were able to catch up to Sony. Due to a bad decision on licensing policies, Sony lost an opportunity to conquer the market, and the Betamax format was finally phased out. A similar erroneous decision brought about the downfall of Apple Computers.

— ADDING LEAD TO GASOLINE

The 1923 corporate decision to add toxic lead to gasoline (to reduce *engine-knock*) changed the chemistry of planet Earth. In 1983, according to the National Research Council (NRC), humans put 363,000 tons of lead into the atmosphere, 75% of it from automobile exhaust. Today we are spending billions of dollars trying to fix the consequences of that terrible decision.

— Kmart

Steve Forbes (CEO of Forbes, Inc.) was reported to have said, "*Today, Kmart is in dire straits because of bad management. In 1991, Kmart had the same sales as Wal-Mart. Ten years later, Wal-Mart had six times the sales of Kmart. Kmart didn't relocate into more profitable areas; they didn't keep up in terms of having good inventory systems—which Wal-Mart did. This was a case of bad management.*"

— Northern Ireland

In 1972, on what is now known as *Bloody Sunday*, British paratroopers opened fire on a crowd in Londonderry, Northern Ireland. While there were many other factors at play, this single bad decision may have led to three decades of some of the worst violence and destruction the world has seen.

I included this extensive list to convince you that we do make bad decisions at all levels.

So Say the Experts!

How often have we relied on experts to guide us? Probably more frequently than we would like to admit; yet, predictions made by many experts have been proven to be erroneous. Here are some examples:

- "There is absolutely no likelihood that man would harness the power of the atom" *(Robert Millikan, German physicist, winner of the 1923 Nobel Prize for Physics)*.
- "Man will never reach the moon regardless of all future scientific advances" *(Dr. Lee de Forest, inventor of the vacuum tube and father of television)*.
- The head of new talent at Columbia Pictures gave actor Harrison Ford a 45-second audition, then told him, "You'll never make it as an actor, stick to carpentry!"
- Arnold Schwarzenegger was told that he should focus on becom-

ing a "personal trainer" as there was no hope for him as an actor. Later, when people said that he had no future in politics, he again proved them wrong.

- Hollywood gurus and media experts predicted that Mel Gibson's "The Passion of The Christ" would be an utter flop. The record speaks for itself—it was a huge success!

- "Atomic energy might be as good as our present day explosives, but it is unlikely to produce anything very much more dangerous" *(Winston Churchill).*

- "This extraordinary monument of theoretical genius (the digital computer) accordingly remains, and doubtless will forever remain, a theoretical possibility" *(Charles Babbage, "father of computing").*

- "The advancement of the art of invention from year to year ... seems to presage the arrival of that period when further improvement must end" *(U.S. Commissioner of Patents, 1844; note that in 1899 the Director of the Patent Office issued a similar recommendation).*

> When a recognized expert says that something is possible, he is almost always right; but when he states that something is impossible, he is likely to be wrong.

Whom can we trust? Well, there is some consolation—we can make an intelligent conclusion from the above experiences (see box).

As General Colin Powell once said, "*Experts often possess more data than judgment.*"

Preconceived Notions

Prior experience and boxed-in notions of what can and cannot be done can be serious impediments to creative or innovative thinking because everyone tends to stay in his/her comfort zone.

Consider the following true events:

— Cliff Young

Australian potato farmer Cliff Young was having a beer at the local pub, when his friends challenged him to run the Sydney to Melbourne marathon (600 miles). In 1983, on the day of the marathon, Cliff appeared at the starter's line. Professional runners had trainers, hi-protein drinks, exotic running gear, stopwatches, charts, etc. Cliff did not even have proper running shoes.

Yet, Cliff won the race easily, and in record time.

What happened here was a classic example of a *boxed-in-belief!* Experts had always postulated that, to survive a grueling marathon, one must run 18 hours and rest for six hours—and everyone subscribed to this dogma. But Cliff had never heard of this. So he ran till he could run no more, then rested for an hour, and ran again; day and night.

The next year, all the runners broke Cliff's record. Why? They all stepped out of the *box*.

— Alcatraz

No prisoner ever escaped from Alcatraz. Each new prisoner was told that he/she could not escape, for three reasons:
  1. One would die of hypothermia in the freezing water.
  2. The swift currents would drag a person to the high seas.
  3. Even if a strong and determined swimmer were to escape the above, the sharks would be waiting.

Today, swimming from Alcatraz to the mainland is an amateur event! How did this come about? People were encouraged to step out of the *boxed-in* belief.

Being closed-minded and resisting change is tantamount to making bad decisions. Here are some preconceived notions that would lead one to poor decisions:

1. Over time, we forget why we do what we do. The same is true of beliefs.

2. We think that what we don't know isn't worth knowing—that it cannot hurt us.

3. For those who built the past, the temptation to preserve it can be overwhelming; we continue to do things because *this is the way we have always done it.* "If it ain't broke, don't fix it" is the worst culprit.

Three

Types of Decisions

*"Never tell people how to do things.
Tell them what to do and they will
surprise you with their ingenuity."*

— GENERAL GEORGE S. PATTON

There are more types of decisions than most people realize. Before you decide on a technique, you need to understand the type of decision warranted. A complicating factor is that marketing gurus are continuously trying to influence your decisions. Below I present some of the more common types of decisions.

Qualitative vs. Quantitative Decisions

If you plan to buy a car, and your primary criterion is *price*, you could gather data on various models and makes, and rank them from cheapest to most costly. This type of information is *quantitative*. Now, if your criterion were the *ride*, you would use your experience to determine whether the ride was rough or smooth, and you would express it in *qualitative* terms.

If you weigh five pieces of quartz, you can determine their weights—this is *quantitative* information. However, if your objective is to use the stones decoratively, you need to rank them *qualitatively,* considering such things as shape, clarity, and color. You have to decide which stones you find more pleasing—this is a *qualitative* decision.

Unique vs. Repetitive Decisions

Decisions may be categorized as *Unique/One-time* or as *Frequent/Repetitive.* As the name implies, one-time decisions require our attention only once. With a repetitive decision, we may still only have to analyze the situation once and thereafter apply our findings repeatedly. For example, once we decide on the optimum route to work, few of us vary it.

It is important to take into account the frequency of a decision, since that will affect our final deliberations and choices. For example, if we go some place once a month, we may select the more scenic route, but if we need to go daily, we may opt for the interstate highway.

Trivial vs. Important Decisions

Which tie to wear is a trivial decision, the consequences of which are not likely to be disastrous. We make such decisions intuitively. Now consider some serious decisions:

- Should we set up a new company or should we acquire a competitor?
- Which contractor is best suited for a specific job?
- Should we lay off staff or rely on attrition?
- Who should manage a particular project?
- How should we allocate funds?

With these types of issues, the consequences of a sub-optimal decision can be quite costly, even disastrous. Of course, a problem that is serious to one person or entity might be trivial to another. An engineer might be trying to decide whether to change jobs, while a CEO may be trying to relocate his company. To each of them, the decision will be crucial—maybe one of the most crucial of his/her career.

Rational vs. Rationalize

Rather than being *rational*, we humans often tend to *rationalize*. To rationalize is to present plausible arguments in order to justify a decision or position.

For example, if we have to take a flight at 8:00 A.M., we may determine that, because of heavy morning traffic and road construction, we need to wake up at 5:00 A.M. This is a *rational* decision, one that is based on a sound analysis of the impact of relevant factors. However, when the alarm rings, we struggle to wake up and, hence, may *rationalize* our need for a little more sleep: today is a holiday so traffic will be lighter than usual. We must be cognizant of the perils of rationalization.

Reacting

Not too long ago, *thinking on your feet* was in fashion. Companies were recruiting smart, young graduates who displayed an ability to discuss a problem intelligently without prior knowledge and without needing to go off and ponder it. I agree this is a valuable skill, but many managers erroneously interpreted *think on your feet* to mean *decide on your feet*. That is a recipe for disaster. Many crucial decisions made without adequate analyses have gone awry. This is akin to a marksman using the *Ready, Fire, Aim* technique.

Soldiers and quarterbacks are required to make decisions in the field without guidance, but the various scenarios and plays have been rehearsed over and over. When under pressure, they do not have the luxury of thinking rationally or analytically—they must react to the situation. Decision-making, however, is not reacting! We should not attempt to mimic this type of response in a business environment. Hopefully, we do not have tin soldiers and armchair quarterbacks running our companies. We must return to the *Ready, Aim, Fire* concept of hitting our target. In decision-making, this translates to *Describe, Dissect, and Decide.*

Contradictory Decisions

The *contradictory* decision is very interesting in that it is made while knowing that we need to act against it.

Many politicians have very good intentions, but because their ability to implement even a small part of their dream depends on winning at the ballot box, they often subordinate their beliefs and say what they think voters want to hear. This is a conscious decision with a hidden agenda.

For example: everyone speaks of wanting peace but, according to the Center for Defense Information,[2] between 1990 and 1999, the U.S. sold arms to 16 of the 18 countries on the State Department's list of terrorist countries. When conflicts arise, many American soldiers are killed with weapons manufactured in the USA. It has been shown conclusively that the cost of crushing terrorism and defusing ethnic conflicts far exceeds the revenue generated from arms sales. So, is this a well-thought-out policy or a lack of clear direction?

President George W. Bush is on a crusade to eliminate terrorism from the face of this earth. It is a very noble cause, and I hope he is successful. Yet, would it not make sense to stop the mass production of arms? Common sense says, "Of course"; but try telling a senator from Tennessee (a state where many gun manufacturers are located) that you want him/her to vote to close down some arms manufacturing facilities. He/she would be *up in arms*—metaphorically speaking.

Many decisions involve such contradictions and, when made unskillfully, they can have disastrous consequences.

Interdependent Decisions

The most obvious examples of *interdependent* decisions are buying/selling and conflict resolution. Negotiations are also a form of buying/selling. Even when both parties are sincere in their desire to reach an agreement, coming to an agreement can often be a challenge. The present Middle East conflict, where Israelis and Palestinians are killing each other even while both desire peace, is an excellent example of how complex *interdependent* decisions can be.

Do not confuse *interdependent* decision-making with *group* decision-making. In *group* decision-making, everybody has the same factors (criteria) and the same options (candidates), and the objective is to reach the optimum solution. With *interdependent* decision-making, participants are not trying to reach the optimum solution, but a solution that is mutually acceptable. As such, *interdependent* decisions are less amenable to mathematical models or tools.

This is why problems among loved ones cannot be solved using decision-making tools. People mistakenly think that they are trying to make a decision, when actually they are trying to come to an agreement. We must be cognizant of the subtle difference. Indeed, it is for this reason that the first step in my 7-step guide is *clearly defining the objective* (see Part II).

The Quick-Fix

Following is an example of a decision that is beneficial in the short-term, but with potentially disastrous long-term consequences.

Imagine the new CEO of a company. Stockholders are looking to him/her to produce an impressive return on their investment (ROI). ROI is defined as the ratio of the numerator to the denominator. The numerator is profits; the denominator is assets, capital, resources, goodwill, etc. Anyone with knowledge of basic math knows that one can increase the ROI by either increasing the numerator or decreasing the denominator.

Being obligated to produce good numbers, the CEO might be tempted to reorganize, lay off personnel, eliminate research and development, and cut projects that will not bring an immediate return. He/she may appear impressive in the short run, but this is a recipe for disaster.

One study of 16 large U.S. corporations indicated that immediately after restructuring, the share-price increased. Three years after the reorganization, however, the average share-prices in all cases were lower than they had been prior to the restructuring.[3]

Another more recent example is the Israeli action in Palestine. The Israelis imposed a siege on many Palestinian cities, even though they [Israelis] were fully cognizant that there was no military solution to the problem. Moreover, they knew that a harsh response to suicide bombings would turn world opinion against them. Nevertheless, the Israelis considered this an important interim measure—*a quick fix.*

Influencing Decisions

Marketing strategists look at decision-making from the other side. They try to influence your decisions to suit their objectives.

We are all accustomed to the endless barrage of advertising via TV commercials, direct mail, telemarketing, billboards, and the Internet. It is amazing how beautiful women, exotic cars, and the image of carefree fun can sell anything. Some of the most creative minds in business are paid handsomely to influence our decisions. They use every clever idea they can generate—from rational to rationalize.

Here are a few examples of other marketing techniques:

— THE HIDDEN COST

The cost of disposal of car batteries and used tires is not included in the price, but is quoted separately; cases for cameras, laptop computers, etc., are sold separately. Similarly, sales tax is not indicated in the advertised price. The average consumer does not think of these additional costs until he/she gets to the cash register.

— THE CASH-BACK TECHNIQUE

Say you plan to buy an automobile for $25,000, motivated by a $2,500 rebate from the dealer. You drive off the lot in a new car with cash in your pocket. It sounds like a winner, but the dealer is actually giving you back your own money. The $2,500 is not a gift, but part of the auto loan on which you have to pay interest! This is an ingenious marketing technique, and it is amazing how many consumers fall for it.

— HOME SALES

The next time you drive around town, pay close attention to the price range marked on the billboards: *Homes from the low $190K to the high $300K.*

This is a well-thought-out strategy. The lower figure is directed at the customer who wishes to get into a high-quality neighborhood and reap the benefit of living in the proximity of higher-priced homes, which would increase the value of his/her lower-priced house. The higher figure is directed at the customer who wants to feel that he/she is in the exotic $300K range, even though he/she might negotiate and finally pay less than $300K for the house.

— 50% Off Gimmick

How often have you seen a product marked "50% off manufacturer's suggested retail price (m.s.r.p.)"?

Let us assume that a retailer's cost of a computer is $1,000. Forget profit—to be able to break even after the 50% discount, the m.s.r.p. must be $2,000—a whopping 100% mark up. The moral—beware of the 50% markdowns and m.s.r.p. They have no bearing on the true price of a product.

— The Price Guarantee

Here is another novel technique. A retailer assures you that if you were to find a better price advertised anywhere else, say within 30 days, he would pay you 110% of the difference. Wow! It sounds like a winner. But let us think about this for a minute.

First—this product is not available anywhere else. For example, Kenmore is made only for Sears, so you will never find a better price. Even brand-name items have different model numbers, for each mega-retailer. Clearly, the guarantee means nothing.

Second—let us say you bought a product for $110.00, and it was advertised for $100.00 at another store. The difference is $10.00; 110% of this is $11.00. For most people, taking advantage of this offer is not worth the trouble.

— The Sears' Brainchild

Of course, we are all aware that products are priced at $3.99 rather than $4.00; $499.99 rather than $500; and $9999.99 rather than $10,000. This was the brainchild of *Sears* and has been adopted by the entire retail industry.

— RETAIL SALES

In the retail industry, marketers try to influence customers to buy their particular products by getting storeowners to give their products greater exposure.

In a liquor store, bottles are stacked on shelves generally five levels high. The bottom shelf is at floor level, requiring a customer to bend down to reach the products, while the products on the topmost shelf are beyond the reach of anyone who is not a six-footer. It is the goal of marketers to get their products placed on the eye-level shelf because those products are spotted first and are easily accessible.

Additionally, marketers prefer to locate their product to the right of the most well-known brands. Why? Because most of us are right-handed. Research into behavioral patterns confirms that the majority of us reach out with our right hand. We tend to grab something that is conveniently placed.

Of course, marketing gurus will continue to come up with creative ways of enticing people to part with their money.

Accidents and Tombstone Technologies

The aviation industry has had the ARS (Accident Recovery System) for several years, but it was only after the 9/11 attack that the FAA required all planes to have this device on board. The ARS would take control of a plane in case it is headed for a crash or a prohibited air space.

Even though we possess the technologies to prevent fatal accidents, we do not incorporate such technologies until disaster strikes. Hence the term "tombstone technologies."

Such techniques and technologies are present in every field, yet the "if it ain't broke, don't fix it" mentality has prevented us from taking action.

Four

Tools and Techniques

"I usually make up my mind
about a man in ten seconds,
and I very rarely change it."

— MARGARET THATCHER

The above quote tells us how even a brilliant leader like Margaret Thatcher made some of her decisions. Sad to say, this is more often the norm than the exception.

Ask any corporate executive about decision-making and he/she will give you the three basic steps:

1. Identify the problem

2. Find the solution

3. Implement the solution

In a broad sense, this is a valid answer, but a closer look shows a fundamental flaw. Though one needs to be cognizant of the implementation phase, implementation itself is not part of the decision-making process. Decision-making is connected to implementation only insofar as seeking options that reflect the goals in terms of time, resources, and being doable.

Furthermore, it is not easy to move from *identifying the problem* to *finding the solution,* which is why I developed the seven-step technique, outlined in Part II.

Experts (in the problem domain) perceive situations in terms of fundamental laws and principles rather than in terms of superficial features. They normally assess a situation rapidly, and decide on a single option, to analyze. If this option is not acceptable, they move to the second option, and so on. Very often, domain-specific knowledge causes biases, and therefore provides a sub-optimal solution.

It is worth noting that *real world decisions* (RWD) are made without choosing among alternatives. The basic mechanism for making RWD is "situation assessment" (discussed later). RWD is often an attempt to formalize and rationalize an already perceived option.

Here I will review the many ways people actually make decisions. After reading this review, you will probably agree that we need a reliable method for decision-making.

Pray to Higher Powers

At one time or another, most of us have prayed for divine guidance. "Please, God," we say, "give me a sign so I will know what to do." This type of decision-making is very personal and is acceptable to many people under certain circumstances. However, we should not try to run our businesses or careers on divine guidance alone. As is commonly said, *God helps those who help themselves.*

Seek Advice from Fortune-tellers

It is now known that Ronald and Nancy Reagan often sought the guidance of astrologers. You may be surprised to learn that some Fortune 500 companies also hire professional astrologers and psychics to help make business decisions. Likewise, law enforcement agencies sometimes seek the assistance of psychics to solve tough crimes.

No one who has studied astrology would contest that there is some validity to this ancient practice. The question is, how consistently accurate are such predictions? Certainly, there have been some very notable successes, but if you read the variety of assertions made every New Year's Day, you will see there are many more failures.

Dictatorial/Monarchical Methods

This is the form of decision-making practised by ruling authorities such as dictators, monarchs, and even certain supervisors. Decisions made in this manner invariably benefit the ruler, while any negative consequences are borne by the populace or the workers.

Egotistical Methods

Egotistical managers abound. Such managers think, with good intentions, that they need to have all the answers and demand to put their fingerprints on every decision. This Mr. or Ms. Know-It-All makes life miserable for others.

Delegate to Subordinates

Delegating decision-making responsibilities is a legitimate practice. Valid reasons for delegating range from time constraints and economics to relying on the person with the most expertise in an area.

There are also some less appropriate reasons for delegating. Some delegate difficult decisions so that they cannot be tied to a bad decision, while still being able to claim credit for a successful outcome. There are also managers who delegate decision-making simply because they are lazy.

Delegation is a necessary management tool, but before delegating, it is wise to ensure that subordinates are adequately trained in decision-making techniques. The knowledge acquired through this book and the use of tools such as *XpertUS* will greatly enhance anyone's decision-making skills.

Pass-the-Buck

This is different from *delegating* in that the responsibility for decision-making is passed up the hierarchy rather than down to a subordinate. Hence, we have the famous phrase, "*the buck stops here.*" The fundamental problem with this is *time.* If the manager or the CEO had the time to make every decision, then there would be no need for intermediate management positions.

Rely on Gut Feelings

How often have you seen a football coach authorize a particular play? If asked, he will say he just had a gut feeling. Sadly, many managers also use this approach. Intuition is important, but if this is one's predominant mode of decision-making, it is a reflection of a dangerous level of overconfidence.

We recall the tragic shooting-down of a civilian aircraft in the Persian Gulf in 1988. The captain of the carrier USS *Vincennes* was informed that radar had detected an approaching aircraft. He had to decide if it was enemy or civilian. He ordered the aircraft be shot down, resulting in the loss of 290 civilian lives. At a subsequent inquiry, scientists informed the Hill Panel[4] that this tragedy could have been averted. The captain had been overconfident about his original decision and had failed to verify critical information about the situation.

Postpone

Postponement can be a legitimate approach to decision-making, especially if the surrounding circumstances are not clear or are constantly changing. Delaying a decision might even resolve the problem.

Most parents get frustrated with the idiosyncrasies of their teenage children, yet many of these problems disappear as the kids grow up.

Another example might be a judge who assigns an offender to psychiatric care for a period of time before making a decision regarding sentencing.

On the negative side, postponing a decision for an extended period can become the same as not making a decision; in fact, the problem might even worsen. Eventually, the passage of *time* will yield a decision.

By Consensus

Many government and semi-government establishments mandate management to reach a consensus; hence they require committees to make certain decisions, some of which are crucial.

The best example of decision-by-consensus is what happens in the U.S. Congress. In business, it is common to see bid evaluation committees, focus groups, and recruiting teams—these are also good examples of forums for this type of decision-making.

I have been associated with a leading energy company where a committee approved all major decisions. In this instance, it was to share responsibility for the decisions. This, in turn, ensured the successful implementation of the decision. However, sometimes this technique is used to ensure that failure is not pinned on any one person.

Follow Established Rules

This type of decision-making is the *modus operandi* of the Armed Forces, police departments and, to some extent, the judicial system. A judge is required to apply the law of the land.

Some businesses or departments are also managed this way, especially when the owners or managers are ex-military personnel.

Pattern Recognition

Even when they use sophisticated computer programs, weather forecasters make their predictions based on pattern recognition.

When the Dow Jones Industrial Average starts to move up, we recognize a pattern and make our decisions accordingly. As with most things, there is a good and a bad side to this. It is certainly wise to perceive patterns, but patterns themselves are not the absolute. Fortunes have been made and lost in the stock market, relying on pattern-based decisions.

Tradition/Superstition

Many people will not fly on Friday the 13th. Even some well-known hotels do not have a 13th floor or a room #13 (triskaidekaphobia).

In many countries, people invite a successful person to visit their homes on the first day of the year, in the belief that this will bring good luck for the entire year. The Japanese, though industrially advanced, pay great respect to tradition in their decision-making process.

When Exxon decided it would drill for oil in Chad (Africa), it had to turn itself into something more than an oil company. It had to become a development agency, a human-rights promoter, a de facto local government and an environmental watchdog. Exxon learned how to build a $3.5 billion pipeline, with the help of NGOs (Non-Governmental Organizations), the World Bank and, yes, chicken sacrifices.[5]

Following a very traditional thought process and basing their decisions on census studies, many companies locate their retail outlets at major intersections. However, basing decisions on tradition can be like wearing blinders—you may be unable to perceive or appreciate new ideas. On the other hand, there are some who have successfully broken away from tradition.

- Sam Walton broke with tradition when he located his *Wal-Mart* stores in unconventional areas—in small towns, as opposed to big cities. What an incredible success this strategy turned out to be!

- While the three major television networks were using highly paid newscasters, CNN decided real-time news was more important than high-profile anchors—another success story.

- Southwest Airlines and a host of other companies have proven that tradition can be a serious impediment to innovative ideas. Pan Am, Braniff, Eastern Airlines, and others went out of business when they failed to innovate.

Many nations are treading cautiously in the face of radical ideas because they fear breaking away from tradition and history. They should recognize that, to some extent, the success of the United States of America could be attributed to the fact that she has no history to hold her back.

Today, we even have a version of English called *American English*, wherein the pragmatic Americans created a workable language out of the *Queen's English*, when no other nation in the world would have dared to touch this sacred heritage.

Gambling

This needs no elaborate explanation. One has only to spend some time in any casino in Las Vegas to observe that few leave as winners.

Heuristics

Heuristics is concerned with figuring probabilities based on what we know. The human mind uses heuristics to think about things that would otherwise be too complicated.

As a test of our preconceived notions, consider the toss of a coin. Students were asked what the probable outcome would be:

A — H T H T T H, or
B — H H H T T T

Nearly 90% of the participants opted for A. Although at a glance A appears to be more random than B, A and B are equally probable.

Decisions based on first impressions fall into this category. Decision-making is not jumping to conclusions, though that is something we have all been guilty of at one time or another, including Margaret Thatcher, former prime minister of Britain.

Decision Analysis

When it comes down to decision analysis, most of us are more preacher than practitioner. Typically, we make a decision and then try to justify it with pseudo-rational arguments. Decision analysis includes the use of mathematical tools. Once we decide to conduct a decision analysis, we must then decide on the methodology and the tools we will use.

Don't underestimate the value of mathematics when it comes to decision-making. People have used mathematics and probability theory to solve many intricate problems. Even though this book is not about the mathematics of decision-making, I strongly urge you to use mathematics wherever applicable.

Life insurance companies, for example, rely on sophisticated mathematical models to arrive at premiums and payouts. They consider criteria such as race, sex, age, demographics, and lifestyle to determine lifespan and premium rates. These methods have served them exceedingly well. Mathematics also ensures the survival of gambling establishments.

Consider this example: As the manager of a candy manufacturing plant, you are required to produce a Valentine's Day candy box. You have to decide its contents, adhering to a set of constraints (see box).

The Candy Box

The base area of the box is 48 sq. inches; the usable area for candy is 83%. There shall be two layers of candy, and the box shall weigh two pounds. You have 48 types of candies to choose from, and they belong to six groups. No single group in the box shall exceed 30% by weight. Candies are of two sizes: 1.1 and 0.7 square inches (base area). The cost and weight of each type of candy are known.

The package will be priced at 400% of the cost of the candies.

There are two goals here:

1. Maximize profitability

2. Provide maximum value to the consumer.

This is a classic problem, which can be solved quite easily using mathematical techniques. Of course, this problem could be further complicated by specifying the maximum cost of material that is allowed in the box, thereby imposing an upper limit on the sale price.

Forecasting

Forecasting is an attempt to predict a future outcome. Whether you use guesswork, gut feelings, astrology, or scientific/mathematical trending, it is highly probable that your forecast will be wrong.

Does this mean that one should not forecast? Of course not! Forecasting is vital in managing decision-making. It provides a framework within which we can act; but if one confuses this with getting a specific answer, one could be in a heap of trouble.

The forms of decision-making discussed above come into play at all levels from the corporate, where millions of dollars are involved, to the personal, where what is at issue might be selecting a college for your son/daughter.

Tools

This section takes a quick look at some of the formal techniques used to aid decision-making. This is by no means an exhaustive list, but represents a few of the more common methods used today.

— DECISION TREES AND THE PROCESS OF ELIMINATION

Decision trees consist of decision *nodes* connected in the form of a tree. At each node a course of action is selected. This method elicits yes/no responses and requires a strict set of rules or conditions. As decision trees do not allow ranking, they are usually of limited value where the judgment is not a straight yes/no. While this process is well suited for automated decision-making, it is highly subjective. Sadly, even these days, many senior executives swear by this technique.

— INTELLIGENT DATABASES

These are computer programs that hold a database of messages. Based on user input, these programs spew out standard phrases that mimic personalized responses. Astrological prediction programs are an example of such a model. They, too, do not allow ranking and are of limited value.

— THE MULTI-ATTRIBUTE THEORY (Pairwise, Scaling and Distribution)

These are dominance search models based on normative theory, as opposed to economic theory. These models are highly applicable to naturalistic decision-making scenarios. Such a technique tries to determine preferences and is used universally in consumer surveys and opinion polls.

— SITUATION ASSESSMENT

1. Concrete information (Problem domain)
2. Context information (Environment)
3. Expertise (The decision-maker)

The case study of the downing of the Libyan airliner (Appendix 2) was analyzed using this technique.

— SERIAL OPTION EVALUATION

Contrary to popular belief, experienced decision-makers do not choose among alternatives. They assess the situation, select a promising alternative option, and conduct a dominance test for validity. If the option fails the test, they select a second option to validate. This is also known as dominance structuring.

— PIECEMEAL EVALUATION

Jurors generally decide on the basis of this methodology. They receive information in small doses, which allows them to develop a scenario.

— ADAPTATION: Imperfect, but important

Both squirrels and humans put away things for safekeeping. Squirrels will bury nuts even in a cage, in captivity, when there are no threats, because it is a genetically inherited program. Humans on the other hand, will adapt to the situation and will not hide their valuables in every situation.

Animals have been known to be very creative as well. Vultures eat dead meat, but one species of African vulture goes for the marrow inside the bone. They carry the bones high up and drop them among rocks to crack them—an extremely creative technique.

— KNOWLEDGE-BASED SYSTEMS

These are a collection of emerging technologies used in reasoning and natural selection. These systems include neural networks, fuzzy logic, evolutionary computation, expert systems, and artificial intelligence, which draw on the advances in neuroscience, cognitive science, and computer science.

Be careful when you select a decision-making tool. Most software in today's marketplace has been developed to address only *quantitative* decision-making needs.

In Appendix 1, I have provided guidelines for selecting a good decision-making tool.

Five

Inherent Limitations

"The conscious mind can hold seven, plus or minus two, pieces of information at a time, either from internal thought or from the external world."

— GEORGE MILLER, eminent American psychologist
(from his famous 1956 paper,
The Magic Number Seven, plus or minus two)

In my twenty years of work in the area of decision-making, I have not found one executive who thinks he/she cannot make a good decision. Of course, many let their boss think that he/she is better at making decisions, and this may be a wise move. There is no doubt that many managers feel they could run the company better than the CEO! We continue to insist that we can make optimal decisions, or even lead a country (see box).

If you are making decisions, it is imperative that you be aware of your own talents and limitations. I urge you to review what you know and update your knowledge. If the need is for knowledge of

The President's Wife

In some developing countries, when the President is assassinated or passes away, his wife takes over the presidency. Does this mean that these ladies were born leaders? Does it mean that they are capable of deciding a country's future? No – but just like you and me, they too feel they know what is best for the nation. Politicians capitalize on the waves of emotion.

a specialized nature, seek the assistance of an expert. I used to manage my own investments and do my own taxes. I learned the hard way and now use professionals for both these functions.

The factors presented below (see box) are inherent limitations of the decision-maker. I will now briefly elaborate on each of these.

Desires/Requirements

A clear objective is half the solution. Before we embark on a decision, we must have a well-defined, unambiguous objective. A vague objective or unreasonable expectations will lead to a sub-optimal decision.

Inherent Limitations

- Desires/Requirements
- Attitude & Expectations
- Mental Limitations
- Personal Circumstances
- Prior Experience
- Fear, Shame & Guilt
- Religion or Faith
- Comprehension
- Frame of Mind
- Overconfidence/Ego
- Knowledge
- Vision & Imagination
- Reasoning
- Memory
- Culture

The vital question is — *why?*

Why do I want to engage in this activity? All too often, people engage in an activity without reviewing the — *why?*

- If you plan to start a business, it is vital that you have a clear idea of your reasons. In a general sense, your objective is to start a business, but for the decision-making exercise, you need to be more specific: i.e. more income; stable income; flexible work hours; less travel; etc.

- Mao Tse-tung opted to employ thousands of Chinese peasants in road-building projects rather than use modern machinery. Even though the Transport Ministry financed these projects, his main objective was not to build roads. He knew that if his people had the dignity of labor and, more importantly, had no idle time, they would have little incentive to engage in protests against his regime. Chairman Mao had a clear objective, though the Western world could not understand it.

• Why buy a cow, when all you need is a glass of milk?

A specific goal or objective has three basic requirements:
1. The goal or objective must be reasonable
2. There should be a time-specific schedule
3. Progress should be measurable

Too often we hear people say, "*My objective is to become rich.*" Can you see the problem with this? It is not specific; we can't measure progress with regard to either time or proximity to success. Is it any surprise that most people with this objective never achieve it? If you cannot measure progress, how will you know if you are on track?

In the corporate world, this would be analogous to the CEO saying to the stockholders, "Our goal is to make a bunch of money!" Of course you never hear that. Why? Because it is neither time-specific nor measurable. You might hear something like, "Our goal is to increase revenue from $2.0 billion to $3.0 billion within 5 years." This is both measurable and time-specific.

Attitudes and Expectations

Even if you have all the facts at your fingertips and everything is in your favor, your decision will be affected by your attitude and your expectations.

- Imagine a general returning from World War II. After fighting in the Pacific, do you think he would be inclined to purchase items labeled "*Made in Japan*"?

- Sit next to a computer programmer and note how he/she keeps complaining that his/her giga-hertz laptop is just crawling. A delay of a few seconds is no longer acceptable. His/her expectations about computer processing speeds have changed, and so will his/her responses to work.

- Many people desire to improve their lifestyle. Yet, they continue to do what they have been doing in the past. For example, let us consider a person who does not go out and meet people but who is desirous of finding a date. He/she cannot expect to find a date unless there is a change of habit and lifestyle. If you continue to do what you have been doing, then you will get the same results that you have been getting. If you have different expectations, you must start doing something different.

Mental Limitations

Professor Miller's work has been well substantiated—our conscious mind has limitations. Be it recruiting an engineer or buying an automobile, we are most certainly affected by our ability to process seven, plus or minus two, bits of information.

This is confirmed by the decision to have 7-digit phone numbers; most people can remember their phone number with ease, but not their credit card number.

Consider judges trying to decide the winner in a beauty contest or an Olympic diving championship. How many bits of data do they have to handle? They must compare many candidates and assign them points, considering the group as a whole. It is a situation ripe for controversy, with a great need for a better form of judging (ranking).

Personal Circumstances

- When you purchase insurance, you choose the deductible. The larger the deductible, the lower the premium. How large a deductible you assume depends on your personal circumstances. In the extreme case, if you can afford to absorb the loss, you might opt to self-insure. After all, what is insurance? It is simply a group of people agreeing to share the losses of one of its members.

Prior Experience

Prior experience (direct and indirect) is immensely valuable in any field.

- NASA (National Aeronautics and Space Administration) sends a crew that combines experienced astronauts and rookies.

- In the NFL (National Football League), teams that win the Super Bowl usually have many players with prior play-off experience.

Note, however, that prior experience can also be a serious impediment to creative or innovative thinking because everyone tends to stay in his/her comfort zone.

Feelings (Courage, Fear, Shame, Guilt, etc.)

Some decisions are driven by shame, guilt, or fear of pain or loss. Here are some noteworthy examples:

- In a TV interview, President George W. Bush admitted that at one point in his life it came down to a choice between Jim Beam bourbon and his wife Laura. His decision to give up alcohol probably had something to do with the *fear* of an immense loss.

- President Bill Clinton stated in front of millions of TV viewers that he did not have a sexual relationship with White House intern Monica Lewinsky. The decision to make that statement was probably rooted in *fear* and *shame*.

- In the late '70s, Jason Metcalf's reckless driving resulted in the death of his pregnant wife. He committed suicide shortly thereafter, leaving behind a letter stating that he was unable to cope with the *guilt*.

Another driving factor in the decisions we make is how we think others might perceive our actions. This is an indirect form of shame, guilt or fear.

- Imagine yourself in attendance at a seminar. The speaker takes a picture of the audience and the attendees each receive a copy of the photograph as they leave. When you receive your copy, who will you look for, first? Of course, you are going to see if you are in the picture! Why? It is human nature to be more concerned about one's self first, before others. So when you make decisions, don't be overly worried about what the other person might be thinking; he or she does not care.

- When the U.S. attacked the Taliban regime in Afghanistan, the media was not granted access because of concern about world opinion.

- Not long ago, a father in Lebanon ordered that his daughter be killed because she became pregnant out of wedlock. He reasoned that the family honor had been tarnished, a crime for which tribal tradition declared the punishment to be death. Fortunately, the girl was able to escape to the U.S. and seek asylum.

Religion and Faith

Many international contracts are lost due to cultural and religious misunderstandings. The impact of religion or faith may not be apparent at first. Since we in the U.S. are averse to inquiring about a person's religion, we never really understand why people think and behave differently. I strongly encourage everyone not only to inquire about, but also to discuss, religion, without fear. Most people are overly eager to explain their faith to others.

- Even though the world's banking system is based on the *time value of money*, Islam prohibits banks and individuals from charging interest on loans. Can you see how this might affect international business transactions? An Islamic nation might decide to use an entity that adheres to Islamic teachings.

We must be respectful of all religions, even though teachings professed by some faiths do not encourage the Western definition of progress and success. Not being mindful of this can hinder good decision-making.

Comprehension (Language) and the Wording Effect

As we know, many decisions are made on the basis of surveys. Why do different surveys yield different results (decisions)?

Let us consider a hypothetical survey question on U.S. policy on terrorism by radical Islamic groups.

All the terrorists who took part in the 9/11 attacks were of the Islamic faith. Thus, to ensure our safety, should we profile all

The Famous Sydney Harbor Bridge

In 1924, Dorman Long (the British iron and steel giant) signed a contract for the construction of a bridge in Australia. When the job was completed, the Australians made the payments in Australian pounds. The British protested; but it was to no avail. The contract did not specify that payment had to be in sterling pounds. Dorman Long suffered a substantial loss.

people of Arabic origin because they are predominantly of the Islamic faith?

Many Americans would respond to this with a resounding YES!

Now, what if we were to reword the question:

Immigrants were instrumental in building America, which has always prided itself on giving sanctuary to people of all faiths. Even though an extremist group of fundamentalist Moslems caused the terrible catastrophe on 9/11, should we selectively profile all people of Arabic origin just because they are also of the Islamic faith?

I am certain that many people who would say *yes* to the first question would say *no* when it is presented in this manner.

Surveys are designed by professionals who understand how to bias the outcome by using appropriate wording. Pay special attention during election campaigns and you will see that the Republicans and the Democrats will often ask the same question and get a different answer. That is because each will use language that favors its agenda.

As well as being an impediment to good decision-making, words can turn out to be very costly—(see box).

Language must always be considered with the utmost care. A few years back, Chevrolet found this out the hard way when they came out with the *Nova.* It was hard to sell in Spanish-speaking countries because in Spanish *No va* means— *it doesn't go.*

Few people recognize the significance of language in decision-making, yet astute professionals, especially those in the legal profession, capitalize on it.

Realizing this, even the White House has been trying to move away from the term *suicide* bombers to *homicide* bombers, a term that leaches the phrase of the glamour of martyrdom.

The Focus

An executive wanted to hire an engineer.

Two groups were asked to review thirty resumes. They were told that it would cost $550 to interview each candidate.

The first group was told to select candidates high on the selection criteria.

The second group was told to reject candidates low on the selection criteria.

The first group selected only 8 to be interviewed, while the second group selected 11.

Surveys have shown that people were more accepting of *80% lean* than of *20% fat,* even though they are the same. Most people use a reference of what is acceptable.

In 1980, UN General Secretary, Kurt Waldheim flew to Iran to negotiate the release of American hostages. At the airport he told a reporter, "I am here as a mediator, to seek a compromise". This was aired on radio, and within 30 minutes, Waldheim's car was destroyed by angry crowds! Why?

In the Persian language: "*to mediate*" is to "interfere or meddle, uninvited", and "*to compromise*" has a negative connotation signifying, "to compromise one's integrity".

Frame of Mind

EXAMPLE A:
You paid $50.00 for a ticket to see a basketball game. When you arrived at the gate, you realized that you had lost the ticket. Would you pay another $50.00 to see the game?

EXAMPLE B:
You decided to see a game with a ticket price of $50.00. When you arrived at the gate to purchase the ticket, you realized that you had lost a $50.00 bill. Would you still buy a ticket?

Where you put the *focus* of a problem also influences the final outcome (see box on page 51).

Frame of Mind

In addition to our values, emotions such as compassion, anger, love, hate, and greed put us in a frame of mind that affects our decisions.

Consider two painters painting the same scene. The first painter has just returned from his honeymoon; the second painter was just informed that his highly opinionated and vocal mother-in-law has arrived for a two-week stay. Do you think their respective paintings, the result of decisions regarding color, theme, and movement, will be influenced by their frame of mind?

In a study, researchers presented two examples (see box) to several groups.

Of the groups that received example A, only 47% said they would be willing to purchase another ticket, while 86% of those who had example B said they would purchase a ticket.

The participants in example A construed that they were paying $100.00 for the game, and many felt that the company should have some way to confirm the sale of the ticket. In example B, the participants were willing to blame themselves for the loss of the money. Note that the financial loss was the same in both cases.

Here is another interesting piece of evidence of *frame of mind.* Nine months after the 1986 World Cup in Mexico, births in Germany dipped significantly. Soccer-crazy German men were staying up late to watch the games, instead of sharing a moment of intimacy with their partners.

Overconfidence and Ego

Overconfidence may be an indication of ignorance or arrogance, but in either case it affects the interpretation of the information presented.

- A mountain climber must consider weather data, his/her endurance level, the logistics, the terrain, and many more variables before making a decision to follow a certain path. The task is never easy, and there are always risks. The climber can easily push the limits of his capability, venturing into overconfidence. Several climbers have perished in the Himalayan Mountains, and it's safe to bet that *overconfidence* was a factor.

- Every year we hear of ferryboats capsizing because those in charge thought they could squeeze a few more people onto a boat that is already full. This is another example of *overconfidence.*

Knowledge

Without a doubt, relevant knowledge has a significant impact on a decision. A person who has studied the stock market will obviously have a tremendous advantage over the less experienced person who is going almost entirely on gut feelings.

If one is not familiar with the subject, it is hard to make a wise choice. To increase the odds of a good decision, one can make the effort to learn about the subject in question, or one can employ cross-fertilization and combine one's own inclinations with the advice of someone who has more experience or expertise.

Vision and Imagination

Certain people are capable of creating a mental image of a problem or a scenario; others are able to visualize solutions. Chess players are possibly the best example of people capable of such visualization. In their minds, they are often ten or twelve moves ahead.

The Rowboat Riddle

A farmer has a dog, a rabbit, and a steak dinner on one side of the river. He needs to take them across to the other side. He has a rowboat in which he can carry only one item at a time. Note that he cannot leave the dog with the rabbit or the steak dinner. So how would he get all of the items to the other side without losing any of them?

(Answer at the end of this chapter)

Reasoning

Reasoning is the process of drawing conclusions from information.

As a simple example, consider the riddle of the rowboat (see box). Note that this problem has very little to do with either mathematics or science. Tests have shown that a person needs above-average powers of *reasoning* to solve this type of problem. However, not everyone is equally skilled at reasoning. Different levels of proficiency in reasoning will produce different levels of success.

Memory

Memory is obviously very important. Knowledge and experience are of little value if one cannot recall the details.

Culture

The most influential factor in decision-making is *culture*. Few understand the profound influence culture has on decision-making; therefore, still fewer people pay adequate attention to culture when making decisions, especially in business dealings.

Cultural decisions are made at two levels: Explicit and Implicit.

— EXPLICIT

Consider these observable behaviors:

- Japanese bow, Arabs kiss, Latinos hug, Asians clasp their hands close to their chest, and Westerners shake hands, all as a form of greeting or acknowledgment.

- Native Americans are often accused of being "shifty" because the Indians will not look people in the eye. Those making the accusations don't realize that in American Indian culture, making eye contact is seen as an invasion of personal space and is reserved for situations of intimacy.

- In the UK, a driver will flash his/her car lights to yield to another driver. However, if a British national driving in Venezuela were to see a flash from a Venezuelan driver and decide to proceed, he/she would be in trouble because in that country a flash signifies—"*I am on the move*".

- A wink of the eye can mean an invitation for a date, dust in the eye, approval of an action, making fun, etc., depending on where you are and the context in which it happens.

- During special holidays, Japanese women give chocolates to men.

- On Valentine's Day, the Chinese do not send roses to their loved ones. Roses die in a few days, while love is meant to last forever.

— IMPLICIT

Implicit assumptions reflect basic conditioning and beliefs.

- For example, European pedestrians would not cross on a red light, even if there were no cars in sight. They just wouldn't do it—they would wait for the light to turn green. On the other hand, in some Central American countries, it is quite common to run a red light.

- In America, fast food is looked down on, but in some cultures eating at a *Pizza Hut* or a *McDonalds* is a show of status. When operating overseas, these franchises locate their restaurants in affluent neighborhoods, while in the U.S. they cater to the less affluent.

- In Germany, the alcoholic beverage Jaegermeister, extracted from a complex mix of 56 herbs, was developed to serve the working class. Yet in the U.S., the name has established itself as a status symbol. There are Jaeger bands, Jaeger T-shirts, etc.

- Also note how status is accorded in different cultures. In the west, status comes from achievement, while in other cultures heritage is more highly valued. In these latter cultures they might ask you who your relatives are, before they inquire as to how you make your living; they might ask where you studied before inquiring about what you studied.

— INDIVIDUAL VS. COMMUNITARIAN CULTURES

Western cultures tend to put a high value on driving a hard bargain, whereas in many indigenous cultures, one ensures status by giving something of even or greater value in an exchange.

In some cultures "greasing the skids" is a commonly accepted practice, whereas in others it is called "bribery" and is illegal. In the U.S., "lobbying" is an approved practice; but many view it as unethical, and even borderline bribery.

The Western notion of *pay-for-performance* has not been effective in communitarian cultures where members do not accept personal recognition at the expense of their colleagues. A well-known U.S. chip manufacturer set up a plant in Malaysia. When performance bonuses were offered to individual members of a research team, the offer was refused. The Malaysians insisted on sharing the award equally among the entire team. Note that the *team concept,* recently in vogue in the U.S., looks somewhat similar, although it is not based upon the same communitarian values that motivated the Malaysians. Rather, in the U.S., management looks to teams to enhance productivity.

Those who live in a communitarian society place a high degree of importance on family and friends, while those who live in individualistic societies tend to place a high degree of importance on

The Saudi Royal Plane

Recently the Saudi ruler visited President George W. Bush at his ranch in Crawford, Texas. It was reported that the Saudis requested the U.S. Federal Aviation Authorities to ensure that no female air traffic controllers were involved in directing the Saudi royal plane. This created a massive backlash from all quarters. How or why should the U.S. react to a request from a foreign nation to violate America's equal opportunity principle?

Since the meeting was to deal with many issues, including the Mid-East crisis, the Iraqi problem, and a possible oil embargo, it was deemed futile to sit on principle and demand that the Saudis give up their position on this.

NOTE: The White House and the Saudis denied that such a request was ever made; but the Union of Air Traffic Controllers confirmed that the request was made in April 2002.

individual success. People in Western cultures are less likely to violate norms to help out a friend, while this is considered an honor in communitarian cultures. Cultural heritage will affect the decisions made by each group.

Today, we live in a global village with many Third-World countries providing cheap labor, subsidized products, and raw materials. Most of all, people in these cultures desire a better quality of life. With the increasing pace of globalization, it behooves corporate management to be cognizant of the tremendous differences in cultures.

Cultural differences can come into play on a local scale as well. For example, there is a wide range of cultural difference just within the United States. People from New England attending a business meeting in California might find themselves overdressed, since West coast culture tends to be much more casual. Forthright New Yorkers might be considered rude in the American South, where there is a stricter code of etiquette, and communication involves reading between the lines.

These types of differences are also prevalent in India, where there are 17 official languages, and scores of different dialects. Cultural differences are probably more pronounced in India than in any other country in the world.

The impact of cultural influence on decision-making cannot be overly stressed. Cultural values may, in fact, be the greatest cause of subjectivity in decision-making. In some instances they take precedence over the most basic of principles (see box).

Solution to the Rowboat Riddle

The farmer would take the dog and leave him on the other side. He would then come back and take the rabbit over to the other side, leave it, and bring back the dog. He would then leave the dog and take the steak to the other side. Finally, he would return for the dog.

Six

External Factors Beyond Our Control

*"What gets us into trouble is not what we don't know.
It's what we know for sure that just ain't so!"*

— YOGI BERRA

In the previous chapter I discussed the decision-maker's inherent limitations—these personal traits are what make people reach different decisions even when they have the same information. The decision-making process is further complicated by external factors, which are often beyond the decision-maker's control.

Material and Physical Resources

When planning projects, it is vital we pay close attention to adequacy of resources.

- The oil boom of the '70s propelled rapid growth in Nigeria. The Nigerian gov-

External Factors

- Material & Physical Resources
- Finance & Economics
- Ideas and Technology
- Military & Management Strength
- Demographics
- Lifestyle
- Regulatory & Policy Changes
- Geopolitics
- Influence of Recent Events
- Competition
- Information

ernment engaged in a massive program to build office complexes and housing. Accordingly, they ordered millions of tons of cement from foreign suppliers. As it turned out, their seaport did not have the capacity (resources) to unload the cement in a timely manner. Ships were on hold for an extended period, and finally many were forced to dump their cement into the sea and continue on their journeys. The cost of demurrage was significantly more than the value of the cement.

Finance and Economics

The industrial growth of the U.S. was fuelled by creative financing techniques. The success of the American economic model stands as a testimony to the significance of finance and economics in decision-making.

- In the past twenty years the U.S. created 55 million new jobs, while Europe, with 30% more people, produced only 10 million new jobs. Britain, in fact, did not have any net job growth at all.

- Where necessary, finance and economics have been used to fight tyrannical empires. America fought Communism for years; yet, it was the economic war that brought down the mighty Soviet empire.

- In its war against Afghanistan and terrorism, America offered financial aid to Pakistan to help fight its economic woes in exchange for support in the war effort.

- On other occasions, the financial might of the Western world has helped countries develop natural resources. A group of large energy companies from the Western hemisphere set up a fund with each contributing about $20 million. This fund seeks to finance energy development programs in Third-World countries and has helped many nations develop projects that otherwise would not have seen the light of day.

Ideas and Technology

Many years ago, policy makers in the Western world, realizing that the oil-rich Arab countries could control the world economy by hiking oil prices and/or reducing production, conceived and executed an ingenious plan.

A Western consortium initiated an energy development educational program. In this program, it was suggested that the oil producers could significantly increase their revenue by selling refined products rather than crude oil. Cheap labor would be available from the poorer neighboring nations, further increasing per-barrel profit. Young Arab managers bought into this idea and convinced the oil sheiks to build refineries and processing plants in their home countries.

But there was more to this recommendation.

In tank farms, crude oil was stored in any available tank. If a tank was partly full, it could be topped-off to fully utilize the spare capacity. However, once they were switched to storing refined products, tanks had to be dedicated to specific products. If a particular product was not sold in time and the tanks assigned to that product were full, the refinery would have to stop refining that product and even shut down. With the refinery at the buyer's mercy, the buyer (often oil companies) dictated prices and terms.

Additionally, you can see how a well-crafted idea/plan resulted in vast opportunities for the Western world:

- Pollution associated with the chemical processes remained outside their territories; it was shifted to the oil-producing nations.

- International contractors got the lion's share of the contracts to build the refineries and processing plants.

- Major Western banks financed the construction programs.

- The big oil companies set up shipping companies to transport the products.

- Western countries developed an entirely new industry to build compartmentalized double-shell tankers.

Similarly, technology gives the decision-maker an enormous edge.

- Until a few years ago there was only one oil company with deep-sea exploration technology. Beyond depths of 6000 feet, there was no competition for this type of work. This company had exclusive rights to this know-how and was able to literally name their price.

- Microsoft vehemently defends its position that the *Windows* operating system is not a monopoly because the consumer can choose another operating system; yet, almost all personal computers come with *Windows* pre-installed. A majority of computers even come with *MS Office* pre-installed. So who would wish to deviate from this technology? Until something replaces the PC, *Windows* is here to stay and will be Microsoft's proverbial cash-cow.

If one does not anticipate technological changes, one might be out of business very soon.

- The vinyl music record is in some museum; the reel-to-reel tape recorder is also history.

- Recognize the name Remington?
  They make shavers and razor blades. They are a well-run company

with a stable market share. Most males shave, though the majority does not particularly enjoy the experience. Researchers have been working for years to develop ways to stunt the growth of facial hair; they know that the solution to this elusive problem is around the corner. Already we have a host of hair-removal techniques. With the recent advances in gene therapy, it won't be long before researchers will find the answer. Voilà! No more facial hair! Men worldwide will rejoice — but not Remington.

Remington does not have a problem at present, but it must be ever-vigilant for potential problems that may arise later. Recently, it has started diversifying.

Military and Management Strength

Often we use the phrase, *negotiate from a position of strength.* If an opponent knows that his/her competitor has the might to impose a decision, he/she will be more accommodating.

- In the late '70s, when the Kingdom of Saudi Arabia threatened to cut off oil supplies to the U.S., President Carter threatened to invade Saudi Arabia and take over the oil production facilities. The Saudis assured the Americans that oil supplies would not be terminated.

- When countries claim that America is a big bully, it is a reflection of America's military might. The truth is that the American military has been the savior of many nations across the globe. Grenada, Kuwait, Panama, and Serbia are just a few examples.

Demographics

In business ventures, it may be prudent to study the demographics. Webster's dictionary defines demographics as *"the dynamic balance of a population, especially with regard to density and capacity to expand or decline."*

- If you were in the high-end jewelry business, you would study census data to obtain the average income in the service area.

- A person setting up a donut shop should be on the right side of the road heading into the business district or industrial area, in order to service morning workers. In fact, as a consultant to such an enterprise, I recommended that they serve ice cream as well. Donuts are popular in the mornings and in the colder months, while ice cream is popular in the afternoons and in the summer. The demand patterns for the two products would provide a steady revenue stream throughout the year.

- The next time you drive, pay attention to where fast food stores are located. Often you will find them very close to one another. In Houston, where I live, there are twelve fast-food restaurants within a half-mile on one street. Likewise, car dealerships tend to be located in the same area. Why? They all use the same evaluation techniques and the same census data. Naturally, they all come to the same conclusion.

It is worth noting that there are companies who challenged this traditional view of demographics and went on to become highly successful. Wal-Mart is a classic example.

Lifestyle

As I pointed out earlier, advances in technology have resulted in the growth of some companies and the demise of others. Furthermore, it has affected our lifestyles. Changes in lifestyle give birth to new opportunities and, directly or indirectly, affect every business.

- Because many of us do sedentary office work, we miss out on physical activities. Consequently, there has been a tremendous demand for gymnasiums and fitness centers.

- With both parents working outside the home, we see a continuing demand for geriatric facilities and childcare centers.

- During the war, in 1942, 900,000 babies were born out of wedlock. While their husbands were away fighting, women went to work and interacted more frequently with other men, which often led to extra-marital relationships.

- The movie industry quickly senses the pulse of the people. In the '50s and '60s, Western movies depicting early American lifestyles were hits, and actors like John Wayne and Clint Eastwood reigned on the silver screen. However, Hollywood has had to cater to changing times and lifestyles. (When was the last time a Western movie won an Oscar?)

- Fashions change from time to time. Certain products lose mass-appeal.

Regulatory and Policy Changes

Regulations and policies are in place to protect society as a whole. Here we are mostly concerned with regulations that govern industries, labor practices and those covering pollution, monopolistic and unfair trade practices. If you are making business decisions, be sure to check out regulatory issues. Even if you are in compliance, evolving changes could pose challenges.

- A friend of mine owned a retail chain which sold fireworks. Recently, the city adopted a new policy banning fireworks within city limits. His sales for the year were down 70%.

- When the Euro was introduced in 2002, many currency exchangers went out of business.

- When the U.S. government ruled Telemarketing to be illegal, many companies faced extinction, overnight! 2 million workers were affected.

- Consider Harley Davidson. Motorcycle sales are at an all-time high. In large part, the appeal of the Harley is the deep, rich guttural sound, which the company even tried to patent as a trademark. Do you think they have contingency plans for the unforeseeable? If a new law were to be passed limiting noise pollution, it would most certainly have an adverse impact on their sales. Harley users like to rev up their bikes—this is an important part of the thrill and the drill.

On the other hand, if your actions are in some way harmful to society, regulators will soon come knocking on your door.

- As an example, consider a large Fortune 500 company that started buying life insurance policies on the senior citizens working for them. It seemed a very nice gesture until it was disclosed that the beneficiary was not the family of the insured, but the company. They had a lobbyist working with the various authorities in each state to get approval. There is nothing illegal about this since the company is paying the premium. What is ugly is that the company was getting a tax exemption on those premiums. This is a case of compliance with the letter of the law, while violating its spirit. It is probably only a matter of time before this loophole is fixed.

- Consider the matter between Kaplan and the Princeton Review (both prepare students for the SAT). The Princeton Review registered the domain name *www.Kaplan.com*. It was reported that, under a threat of litigation, the president of Princeton Review offered it to Kaplan for a case of beer. The matter was resolved without much ado.

Occasionally, there are instances when the government has to curb abuses by large organizations. In these instances, government intervention is mandatory.

- The government reprimanded a mega-retailer (a Fortune 500 company) for unfair trade practices when the company sold drugs below cost until the smaller pharmacies were unable to compete, and then promptly increased prices.

- During Microsoft's anti-trust suit, it was alleged that Microsoft used unfair tactics in an attempt to bring down Netscape.

In both of the above cases, these companies made decisions in compliance with the law; but the intent and the spirit were probably ignored.

Geopolitics

It would be erroneous to think that international actions have no bearing on your home-based business. Nothing can be further from the truth. We live in a global economy with barriers tumbling every day. The war on terrorism has obviously affected all facets of decision-making, be it business or personal.

- In the days of the British Empire, one could not have imagined the day when a citizen of another country would be able to live and work in Britain without any restrictions; but as a member of the EEC, Britain had to open the doors.

- Every large American manufacturing company has set up facilities in less developed nations because of cheap labor and/or resources.

- President Clinton helped avert a collapse of the Mexican economy because it was not just Mexico's problem. The U.S. would have had to deal with the fallout from such a collapse.

Influence of Current/Recent Events
Also known as the *Anchoring Principles*

- After an earthquake or flood, people flock to purchase insurance; yet, a year or so later, most forget completely the need for insurance.

- After the 9/11 attacks in the U.S. and the subsequent anthrax scare, doctors' offices were flooded with people wanting to be tested for exposure to anthrax. Six months later, anthrax was old news, and concern abated.

Competition

Competition is a reality. If it is not present now, it will surface shortly. Many do not realize that frequently we invite or encourage competition by our own actions. Consider the following examples:

- The rulers of Abu Dhabi, Bahrain, Qatar, and Oman are equal partners in Gulf Air, formerly the only international airline in the Middle East. Dubai, also a member of the Gulf States, lacked an airline of its own and requested to join the partnership. The owners refused.

Not to be humiliated, Dubai formed its own airline. The rest is history. Emirates Airline has won the *best airline* award several times, and Dubai has become the de facto transit hub between Europe and Asia. The new Dubai airport is an architectural marvel. Emirates Airline has become the primary choice for travel between Europe and Asia, while Gulf Air has been relegated to the position of a second-class carrier.

- Microsoft wanted to partner with EB (Encyclopedia Britannica) to develop an encyclopedia on a CD-Rom. Since EB did not show an interest, Microsoft developed Encarta with another company. With the proliferation of personal computers, few consumers are in the market for expensive, cumbersome volumes that quickly become outdated. It is only a matter of time before we see the demise of another household name, unless EB reinvents itself. A bad decision can wipe out a corporation.

- During the 1970s, when OPEC (Organization of Petroleum Exporting Countries) started raising the price of oil, people began turning to alternate energy sources. Today, Europe produces a substantial portion of its electrical energy from nuclear power plants. If the oil cartels had kept their greed in check, Europe would still be using oil to generate electricity and the high demand for oil would have continued.

The presence of competition accelerates the need for many decisions. Some people think nothing can be done about a competitor other than to engage in a price war or an advertising campaign, but a little creative thinking would help generate other options.

Some of the options we can use to nullify competitive threats are:
- Improved quality
- Creative marketing
- Technological innovation
- Superior customer service.

Another effective way to thwart competition is to change the rules of the game by setting new standards or creating new requirements. If you are the first to change the rules, you have the knowledge and the resources to play by them. Competitors have to learn the new rules and build the necessary infrastructure to play by them. This gives you the edge. By the time the competitor gets into the game, you can change the rules again, thus always staying in the lead and setting the pace. Few strategists ever consider this option because it requires a thorough understanding of the business and bold, innovative thinking.

This technique has helped the auto industry fight counterfeit parts manufacturers from Asia. With each new model, automobile manufacturers change the designs of fast-moving parts. This makes it almost impossible for the pirates to stay abreast since it is uneconomical for them to make new molds and/or re-tool each time a new design is introduced.

In fact, automobile manufacturers went much further to grab a share of the lucrative service business itself.

- First, they tried to keep the repair business confined to the dealerships.

- They then set up their own outside service outlets, such as Mr. Goodwrench.

- Now, some manufacturers are withholding diagnostic codes required to identify specific problems. The companies have defended their actions as being *safety-related*. Of course this had serious repercussions, notably consumer frustration. However, under pressure from consumer groups and government agencies, manufacturers have agreed to release all codes.

Priceline (the airline ticketing company)[6] is a classic example of changing the rules. They revolutionized the airline ticketing business. Today the consumer can decide what he/she wants to pay for a ticket. Additionally, Priceline patented all aspects of their system, thus guaranteeing a virtual monopoly for many years to come.

Context

The context in which a decision is made has a significant impact on the final decision.

On February 21, 1973, when a Libyan airliner flying from Benghazi, Libya, to Cairo, Egypt, strayed into the Israeli-occupied Sinai Peninsula, two Israeli F-4 Phantom Fighter jets were dispatched to intercept the airliner. After a series of warnings, the F-4s forced the airliner to crash-land; sadly all but 1 of the 123 passengers perished.

The investigation that followed concluded that this tragedy could have been avoided.

Undoubtedly, if this had been a German airliner entering airspace over France (a friendly country), it would not have suffered this fate. (Refer to Appendix 2 for more details.)

Information

The factors I discussed above reach the decision-maker in the form of information, which needs interpretation. It has often been said that *management is making decisions with incomplete information.*

While information without ideas can be useful, ideas without information are worthless. Most people erroneously think that gathering information will eliminate the need for ideas.

Information is like a map—it requires interpretation. A map is not the territory, but a representation of it that allows us to conceive the territory. Once again, this interpretation opens the door to subjectivity. It is imperative that decision-makers consider the following when analyzing information:

— INVISIBILITY

Sometimes we do not see the information, either because we are wearing blinders or because we do not recognize the relevance of such information.

- The principal function of the CIA is to gather bits and pieces of information and identify plausible scenarios, invisible to the layperson.

— IMPOSSIBILITY

At times, the facts are before us, but we do not react to what we see due to our trust and belief in history and experience. The facts are not invisible; we see them, but we do not believe.

- Before the 9/11 attacks on the USA, there were many signs that terrorists were gradually increasing their activities. Yet, the White House and the intelligence agencies thought that an attack against the U.S. mainland was an impossibility.

- Even the FBI fell victim to *impossibility*. For two decades, Robert Hanssen, the most notorious spy traitor, was passing top-secret information to the Soviets. In spite of his access to sensitive material, he was never polygraphed or interviewed. Even after evidence of a mole surfaced and the subsequent arrest of the CIA's Aldridge Ames, the FBI did not pursue other leads because they thought it was impossible that Hanssen was a traitor. The FBI is still trying to determine the extent of the damage to the U.S. security apparatus.

- Similarly, many companies have failed because they did not admit to themselves that the competition was breathing down their neck. There is a plethora of examples that illustrate this point: IBM vs. Microsoft; Xerox vs. Canon; Continental vs. Southwest Airlines; Smith Corona vs. Brother; General Motors vs. Toyota.

— APPLICABILITY

We think we can make straight-line projections from historical data. Because of our passionate attachment to what we know from past experience and/or general knowledge, sometimes we actually believe that we can fit a square peg into a round hole.

- Just because house prices in your state are predicted to rise by 20% next year, you should not assume that prices in your neighborhood would follow suit.

— ACCESS

All too often we do not have access to relevant information. It is imperative that you seek every avenue to get such information. You will be pleasantly surprised to find that all you have to do is ask. The Internet is indeed ideal for information-gathering.

— AUTHENTICITY/CREDIBILITY

Unfortunately, most information used in decision-making is neither complete nor quantitative; hence decisions have to be made under difficult conditions. The lower the quality of the available information or the lower our confidence in that information, the more subjective decision-making becomes.

When making a decision, how frequently do people ask:
- Who supplied this data or information?
- Does the provider have a vested interest in the outcome?
- Is the information accurate?
- Is the information outdated?

It is shocking how many decisions are made without paying attention to such details.

- Situations involving information management at major corporations such as Enron and WorldCom have recently come to the forefront. The price of a stock is highly sensitive to quarterly earnings. Therefore, a CEO tries to either under-report in a successful quarter or inflate earnings (by borrowing from future earnings) in a bad quarter. Thus, CEOs can easily manipulate earnings data to suit their objectives; this is known as *earnings management*. It is unfortunate that we cannot trust information provided by some of these reputable companies. It is a case of buyer-beware.

- A recent study revealed that coconut oil was harmful to humans. Who sponsored the study? A British palm oil marketing consortium! Often when we hear of a study that recommends a particular drug, we find that its manufacturer is the study sponsor. I am not saying that this is false information, only that it is important to be cognizant of the source of the information and to seek independent verification.

- Until very recently, the U.S. government denied the existence of the Army's "Delta Force".

- It was only in 2002 that the U.S. government acknowledged the existence of "Area 51", a top-secret testing facility—in spite of the many photographs that showed its existence.

Seven

Thinking Creatively

"You see things, and ask—why?
I dream things and ask—why not?"

— George Bernard Shaw

We humans are innovators by birth, but conformists by training!

Avid fishermen, Jack and Joe are fishing in a pristine river, in the Pacific Northwest. Suddenly, Joe observes an angry grizzly bear coming at them from the other side of the river. The two friends run toward land.

The role of creativity is that of generating and identifying options with which to solve a problem.

The role of decision-making is that of ranking options, and selecting the optimum.

Once on land, Joe takes to his heels, while Jack sits down to remove his wading boots and put on his sneakers. Joe shouts, "Jack, you fool, what makes you think you can outrun that grizzly simply because you put on a pair of sneakers?"

Jack smiles and replies, "Who said I had to outrun the grizzly…. I just have to outrun you".

Jack thought creatively! Jack survived! In today's competitive environment, you cannot survive on sub-optimal decisions.

Conform!

— At home, we were encouraged, rewarded, or forced to conform to traditions, to what our parents considered norms and values.

— At school, we were stereotyped to do what educators thought was good for us.

— At work, we are required to comply with mission statements and corporate policies.

Much has been written about exploring the many forms of creative thinking. In his book, *The Art of Thought*,[8] Graham Wallace describes the creative process as *preparation, incubation, illumination,* and *verification.*

Creativity plays a major role in decision-making, but being creative does not guarantee that one will make the best decision. By the same token, even the best decision-making tools, techniques, and skills are useless unless you have developed innovative options from which to find the optimum solution. This is why creativity is so important to good decision-making.

Creativity is concerned with change, innovation, inventions, new ideas, and challenging the status quo. To be creative you may need to be a *rule-breaker,* but this is not easy since it goes against our entire upbringing. When we were growing up we were taught to conform (see box). Now we are being asked to be *creative,* to think of something that is not intuitive—what a contradiction!

Tell a young American college graduate to think of a way to trap a monkey. He/she will come up with many ingenious ideas, all based on some type of device. Yet farmers in Africa have been using an extremely creative way to catch monkeys. They dig a hole in the ground with an opening just large enough for the monkey to grab the food they place inside. The monkey cannot withdraw his hand unless he drops the food, which he will not do. This is an extremely creative idea; the farmers use the monkey's natural behavior to trap him.

During the Vietnam War, the U.S. Air Force continuously bombed the North Vietnamese bridges in an attempt to thwart the movement of men and machines to the war front. The U.S. could not understand how the Vietcong kept moving forward in the face of such an incessant bombing campaign. It was later revealed that the Vietcong built their bridges just below the water line so that the U.S. planes would not be able to spot them. This was the creative idea of a young soldier.

The Bus Stop Problem

Imagine you are driving along on a wild, stormy night. As you pass by a bus stop, you see three people waiting for the bus:

1. An old lady who is very ill;

2. An old friend who once saved your life;

3. The perfect man or woman you have been dreaming about.

Knowing that only one passenger can fit in your car, which one would you choose?

Hint: Clearly identify your objective.

(Answer at the end of this chapter)

The best way to illustrate creative thinking is through an example, which was presented at an interview (see box—the bus stop problem).

———

We are continually confronted by great opportunities brilliantly disguised as insoluble problems. Opportunities abound if one can only see them.

A baby learns quickly because he/she does not have to unlearn anything. Adults generally work in an area where they have expertise. Living in the safety and comfort of what they know, they are often reluctant to unlearn things that have served them well. Consequently, they are slow to learn and slow to make progress. An organization (i.e., the individuals who make up the organization) must unlearn some of its past before it can think creatively. To speed up this process, many companies cross-fertilize by bringing in talent from other industries.

Creative thinking is greatly enhanced by cross-fertilization of talent.

Truly creative and unique ideas go through three stages—
1. Initially ridiculed.
2. Then violently opposed.
3. Finally accepted as self-evident.

Creative thinking helps us identify mega opportunities.

How did Canon take away a huge market share from Xerox? They identified the business model that Xerox was using to generate revenue—leasing, as opposed to selling, copiers. As Canon sought strategic options to compete with Xerox, most of the options proposed revolved around creative leasing and financing techniques. Yet, from these sessions, which began with a focus on the competitor's strategy, a revolutionary idea was born: build an inexpensive *personal* copier, thereby eliminating the need for leasing. When Canon considered building a copier that would sell for less than $1,000, initial reactions were: *that's ridiculous, impossible, preposterous,* etc. But Canon's management had the courage and the wisdom to follow through with this groundbreaking idea. The rest is history; the idea turned out to be an enormous success.

How did Microsoft, Dell Computers, Wal-Mart, CNN, and Charles Schwab take on the giants in their respective industries? They came up with creative ideas. Each broke away from tradition to become a giant in its own right.

I present herein three well-known techniques for generating creative ideas. Most other creativity-generating techniques are simply offshoots of these three. The first is a group effort, while the second seeks to stimulate the creative genius within the individual. The third is one that I developed to help find every available option.

1. Brainstorming and Cross-Fertilization — Creativity Through Group Interaction

Alex Osborne first wrote about *brainstorming* in his 1953 book, *Applied Imagination*.[9] Every large business entity has used brainstorming to arrive at creative solutions. Its power is in the cross-fertilization of knowledge and experience gained from people of diverse backgrounds, especially those without any knowledge of the subject under consideration.

Beware! Brainstorming is not Focus Groups.

- Focus Groups rarely produce any revolutionary ideas!
- Brainstorming stresses *quantity* of ideas, while Focus Groups seek *quality*.
- *Control-freaks* and *Loud-mouths* dominate Focus Groups.
- Ideas rarely follow good thinking; ideas follow *power*.

If not properly managed, a brainstorming session will degenerate into a Focus Group.

Cross-fertilization is so fundamentally important that universities have a policy of maintaining ethnic and cultural diversity to ensure that young minds are revitalized through interaction with diverse views and values. To see the value of cross-fertilization in history, look at civilizations like the Aztecs and Mayans, which were eventually wiped out because they were closed societies.

The advertising industry generates some of the most creative ideas. Another group who are creative are comedians. They are constantly involved in finding creative ways of entertaining us. In fact, I have invited both groups to brainstorming sessions, and found the experience to be very effective.

At a recent brainstorming session where the objective was to find a way to increase potable water in Saudi Arabia, one suggestion was to float icebergs (an iceberg is made up of fresh water) to Saudi Arabia. Need I tell you the reaction? This idea was subsequently studied at length and, even today, it remains a viable option for the Saudis.

Sony Corporation spent an enormous amount of resources developing a robot for industrial use. Yet the robot did not gain much acceptance due to its unpredictability. Brainstorming led to the decision to market the robot as a toy; this led to the creation of AIBO, a very cute dog. Unpredictable behavior of a toy is considered funny, but this is not the case in industrial applications.

Brainstorming is sometimes referred to as "Divergent Thinking", and the final analysis is referred to as "Convergent Thinking". In Appendix 3, I provide a detailed breakdown on how to conduct a brainstorming session.

Cross-Fertilization

Cross-fertilization is the most significant driving force responsible for the huge leaps in research and development. Advances in the info-tech industry have made it possible for specialists from areas such as wireless computing, cognitive computing, sensors, genotyping, bionics, biofuel, quantum nucleonics, nanotechnology, high-performance materials, etc., to join forces to achieve impressive breakthroughs.

Examples of cross-fertilization abound in the corporate arena:
- British Airways hired a marketing manager from Mars (the candy manufacturer).
- Home Depot enticed the man behind the success of IKEA.
- IBM was struggling when they brought in Lou Gertsner from RJR Nabisco; this turned out to be a brilliant strategy.

- AT&T hired Michael Armstrong away from Hughes Electronics—a winner!

In a more recent case (2002), Rick Wagoner, CEO of General Motors, recruited Bob Lutz, a design executive of Chrysler Corporation, and John Devine, a former Ford Motor Company finance guru, probably to power up cross-fertilization.

However, the greatest example of the success of cross-fertilization is the United States of America. Immigrants of diverse cultures from all over the world joined forces to make America what it is today: an economic and military superpower; a champion of democracy and freedom.

Most executives rarely venture into the unknown because of a lack of vision, inherent conservatism, or fear of failure. Before they take a step in a new direction, they will ask the proverbial question, *"Has it been done before?"* This is a very valid question, which should be asked; but one should not be afraid to engage the unknown. One should not shy away from an opportunity simply because something has not been done before. If it is a pioneering effort, the decision might merit further scrutiny; however, a decision should stand on its own merit, and not rely on history. When it comes to decision-making, management falls into one of two groups.

In the first group are the followers—the *cows* (*cows follow the one in front*). They will:
- Buy a stock once it has started its upward movement.
- Invest in property after prices have already escalated.
- Open a branch office after a competitor has cornered the market.
- Launch a new product after a competitor has proven its viability.

Sadly, there are many among our ranks who live by the "if it ain't broke, don't fix it" mantra. In their world, everything is at a standstill;

nothing needs to be improved; there is no need for inventions. They will certainly fade into extinction before long!

In the second group are the *seals* (*after the Navy Seals*). These folk have been trained to evaluate a situation and be the first to make a move. *Seals* recognize that the best opportunity for an attack often lies in uncharted terrain.

A classic example is the recent mergers among the giant oil companies. In December 1998, BP and Amoco merged; this had the others wondering about BP-Amoco's strategic thinking. This was followed by the Exxon-Mobil merger; a year later Chevron and Texaco announced merger plans. On the international scene, Total and Fina merged, and soon TotalFina merged with Elf Aquitane.

Not to be left behind, Conoco and Phillips merged [2002], and finally Shell Oil Company acquired Pennzoil.

I wonder how many of these mega-decisions were prompted by aggressive strategic thinking, and how many were defensive plays.

Banking and finance industries also consolidated as soon as the Glass-Steagle Act, which kept commercial banks, investment banks and insurance companies from competing against each other, was repealed. Citicorp merged with Travelers. Not to be left out, Chase merged with J.P. Morgan.

When an opponent takes a position, you should not scornfully disregard it as a foolish move, but rather visualize what made him/her act in that manner. I have seen many executives denigrate an idea because they felt bad about not having thought of it first.

2. Lateral Thinking (Thinking Out-of-the-Box)

Dr. Edward de Bono first developed *lateral thinking* and is the author of many books on the subject. Lately, it has become fashionable to refer to lateral thinking as thinking *out-of-the-box*.

Lateral thinking, like brainstorming, has a huge influence on decision-making. If you do not have a viable list of options, no tool on earth can produce a good decision. Therefore, I cite several noteworthy cases where lateral thinking produced ingenious solutions. Hopefully, you will develop the vision and the courage to *boldly go where none has been before.*

— THE INTERNET

The Internet, in itself an incredibly creative concept, has generated some very creative ideas. Who would have imagined that we would get search engines, e-mail services, web-hosting services, individual websites, etc., free of charge?

— TIMESHARING

Owning one week of a vacation home is a truly creative idea.

— BARNES & NOBLE

Barnes & Noble pioneered the concept of encouraging customers to sit comfortably and browse through books before buying them. Previously, this was unthinkable. Today, other large booksellers, such as Borders, have adopted this concept.

— THE FOSBURY FLOP

Olympic high jumper Dick Fosbury came on the scene with a backward flop, now known as the *Fosbury-flop*. Previously, all high jumpers used a technique called the *barrel-roll*. Fosbury started doing something different when he was still in high school. He turned just as he approached the bar and flung his body backwards. Many tried to dissuade him, but today the *flop* is the technique of choice in high jumping, and has probably increased the earlier limits by at least 12 inches. The *flop* was not just better, it was dramatically better.

— SERVICE MERCHANDISE

Every retail store follows the same procedure: you pick up the product and take it to the counter, make the payment, and carry it to your car. Service Merchandise stores deviated from this practice. At Service Merchandise, you pick up a product card and take it to the cashier. On completion of payment, the order is automatically transmitted to the storage area. When you go to the pick-up counter, your product is waiting for you. The concept was a real success. Note, however, that due to other pressures, all Service Merchandise stores closed their doors in early 2002.

— WAL-MART

Recall the example used in our discussions on fast-food restaurants and demographics (p. 64). Most retail stores, except Wal-Mart, use a similar model for determining optimum location. In his wisdom, Sam Walton opted for a different model. He saw things laterally. He said, *"I am willing to serve a market where there is a need; where the customer is,"* and originally located his stores in small towns. Today Wal-Mart stores are everywhere, even in large metropolitan areas.

— MANAGING COMPETITORS

A friend of mine manufactures airbrushes (which include a compressor), and has 80% of the market share. Recently, his only competitor decided to discontinue manufacturing a rival airbrush because the cost of his compressor was too high. At this point my friend came up with a very creative solution. Rather than gloat at the demise of the competitor, he offered to provide his competitor with a compressor at a very affordable price! Why?

It was better to keep this (known) competitor, who was content with a 20% market share, in business, rather than provide an opening to a new competitor, who might be tempted to aggressively go after capturing a greater market share. This was a brilliant move—a result of a lateral thinking effort.

— THWARTING ANIMAL INSTINCTS

Indian peasants collecting firewood in the forests were being attacked from behind, by Bengal tigers. Recognizing that tigers do not attack from the *front*, the peasants came up with a very creative solution. They wore capes that had the face of a human painted on the back.

— ADVERTISING

In 1975, German and English soccer champions met at Wembley Stadium in London for the traditional clash of the giants. However, TV stations declined to show the game, as there were too many billboards around the playing field; they claimed that this was a major distraction. There was a serious impasse.

Jaegermeister, the German liquor manufacturer, came up with an ingenuous solution. They purchased the advertising spots from all the German advertisers, painted the billboards *white,* and left them blank. This resulted in a publicity bonanza for

Jaegermeister; they got national and international media coverage. Additionally, every time the camera focused on a blank billboard, the commentators referred to Jaegermeister.

— DRUG ENFORCEMENT AGENCY (DEA)

For years the U.S. government has been battling the problem of drugs, not only within its borders, but also in other countries. Caspar Weinberger (U.S. Defense Secretary, 1981-87) courageously suggested the legalization of drugs in order to take the economic incentive out of drug trafficking. No one has had the political will to test his theory. The DEA does not support this theory; they must truly believe that it would not yield the desired results. On the other hand, if drugs were to be legalized, there would be no need for the DEA. Recently the Canadian government started a limited program to legalize drugs. The state of California has also locked horns with the federal government on this issue. Interestingly, marijuana is legal in the Netherlands.

— NETWORK MARKETING

Consider the conventional retail-marketing concept. Goods move from the manufacturer, to wholesaler, to distributor, to retailer, and finally to the consumer. Including the three transporters in between, a total of seven entities marks up the price of the product. Typically, the manufacturer gets only 18–20 cents of every dollar spent at the cash register.

Network marketing brings the goods directly from the manufacturer to the consumer. The consumers themselves are the distributors. All the intermediaries are eliminated.

Sadly, there have been abuses in this industry. The Amway Corporation is the premier network marketing company—the standard by which others are measured. There are many Amway millionaires, thanks to the Amway Corporation, which has given stability and credibility to this industry. Today, Amway products are distributed through Quixtar, which capitalizes on the power of the Internet.

In Part IV, I present some examples to help you further explore lateral thinking.

Lateral thinking is creative thinking. However, lateral thinking and conventional creative thinking are somewhat different. The creative skills an artist possesses are not helpful in lateral thinking. An artist's perception is certainly different, and beneficial to society. However, an artist is channeled in his way of perceiving, and is unable to think laterally. Lateral thinkers have diverse experience and are multi-talented. Most of all, they are not bashful at proposing seemingly preposterous ideas. Indeed, truly creative solutions are born of such ideas.

3. The "AIM-PRESET" Technique

Fortunately, it is possible to learn to think laterally/creatively. Here is a simple method that will help you explore all possible options to solving a problem. It has the acronym *AIM-PRESET*, which stands for: *Accept, Isolate, Modify, Problem, Replace, External, Sacrifice, Environment,* and *Time*.

These are the basic questions you should ask each time you are faced with a problem. With every problem you face, employ the *aim-preset* technique to search out your options. This requires you to spend some time thinking through the implications. Do not jump at what comes naturally. Many are inclined to charge at a problem like a *cavalry*; the *aim-preset* technique is akin to *artillery*, where you search out the coordinates.

Use each of these questions to probe deeply into a problem, and you will be able to generate creative solutions. However, before you engage in this exercise, be certain that you are clear about your objective. Remember, an optimum solution can be found only after the objective is clearly defined.

I have cited examples where the *aim-preset* technique is applicable. Once you identify the options, you would use a technique such as *XpertUS* to determine the optimum.

Beware! Often you might see only the negative side of a changing scenario. Keep focusing on the problem, occasionally changing the focus in order to open your eyes to benefits that may outweigh any potentially harmful consequences.

For example, consider the nightmare of killer bees. Coffee growers in Brazil are happy about the presence of the killer bees, while the rest of the Americas are fighting to wipe them out. Why? Coffee plants pollinated by these bees have increased their yield by about 50%. This emphasizes what I have said before—which solution you seek or adopt depends on your focus and/or objective.

A — Can I simply accept the problem and learn to live with it?

We need to figure out if the problem is worth fixing, or if the solution is cost-effective.
- Your company relocated, adding an extra half-hour to your commute. Is this worth looking for a new job closer to home, or can you live with it?
- You purchased a new home and the family budget is under strain. The family must decide if the parent who opted to take care of the kids should go back to work, or if they would accept the loss of some leisure activities.
- In a marital relationship, there are often disagreements and differences. Every day, couples are deciding whether to live with differences and problems, or whether they should separate.

I — Can I isolate the product or the system from the harmful influence?

Most security systems are based on this theory.
- Firewalls are built around computer networks to thwart hackers.
- Fences are installed to keep out unwanted visitors.
- When x-raying a patient, the dentist places a lead apron (shield) on the patient to reduce exposure to radiation.
- Book covers are laminated for better protection.

M — Can I modify the product or the system?

Product modification is possibly the most common solution.
- If you take chocolates from Europe to a country such as Nigeria, the chocolate will melt at ambient temperature. Chocolates purchased in Nigeria, however, will not melt because manufacturers add ingredients to alter the melting point of the chocolate, thus modifying the product.
- When tires showed excessive wear, manufacturers modified the rubber compounds with synthetic additives to increase the wear resistance.

- Because pure gold is too soft, it is alloyed with other metals to give it the desired hardness.

P — Is it possible that the solution might be in the problem?

Can we turn the problem into an *opportunity?*

- Vaccines are derived from the source of the problem.
- In 1984, Jack Valenti, chairman of the Motion Picture Association of America, objected to the VCR, claiming that its impact on the movie industry was like the *Boston Strangler was to a woman home alone.* Hollywood entrepreneurs have since learned to convert their worst nightmare into a golden opportunity. Today, VHS and DVD sales account for nearly one-third of Hollywood's revenue.
- When monkeys were bothering farmers, they used the monkeys' own habits (refusing to let go of food) to trap them.
- One of the lesser-known dangers of earthquakes is the release of lethal radon gas as the earth's plates spread open. Today, in addition to studying ways to deal with this problem, physicists are trying to predict earthquakes by studying the presence and the rate of release of radon gas, thus converting the problem to an opportunity.
- Many years ago, rodents infested certain areas of England, destroying crops. The rodents were the *external* cause of the problem. Laboratory tests showed that a high-frequency sound generated at night caused the rodents to suffer epileptic fits and die. The rodents' biological clock triggers a protective mechanism that makes them immune to noise during the daytime; somehow, this protection is rendered ineffective at night.

R — Can I degrade the product and replace it?

More and more manufacturers are resorting to this technique to cut costs and ensure a constant demand for their products. The downside is the cost to the environment.

- Disposable razors, plates, and even cameras are good examples of this type of solution.
- Rather than retrofitting, manufacturers are choosing to trash millions of obsolete cellular phones, thereby creating a major environmental problem.

Often the cost of repairing something exceeds the cost of replacement.

E — Can I eliminate or mitigate the external cause of the problem?

- Use of insecticides.
- If you have a disruptive player on your team, you have the option of removing him/her from the team.

S — Can I use direct or indirect sacrificial techniques?

- When the *re-entry vehicle* (which brings the astronauts back to earth) enters the earth's atmosphere, it encounters extremely high temperatures. NASA engineers sacrifice the outer shell of the vehicle to get through this heat window.
- A similar technique is used in cathodic protection of pipelines. A sacrificial anode is destroyed in order to protect the more valuable pipeline.
- In automobiles, brake-shoes are sacrificed to protect the more expensive metallic parts.
- In war, we consciously sacrifice soldiers for the good of the nation.

E — Can I change the environment in which the problem thrives?

- Genetic modifications to plants prevent certain pests from residing in them.
- Chlorine is added to potable water to kill certain bacteria.

T — Will the passage of time resolve the problem?

Time is a valuable tool in resolving problems. When we are annoyed, we need some time to cool down. So why not use this as a tool for problem solving?

- Parents go through some very difficult times with their teenage children. Some parents get frustrated and resort to all sorts of remedies. Others take a philosophical attitude and accept this as a passing phase in a teenager's life.
- The kids are growing up, and the house feels too small. You can move, or renovate to create more space. But since in six years or so the kids will be gone, should you bother?
- Farmers rely on *seasons* (time) to maximize their yield.

Other Creative Thinking Techniques

Over the years people have developed a variety of techniques such as: Mind Mapping; Problem Reversal; Ideatoons; DOIT; LARC; Metaphorical Thinking; The Lotus-Bloom Technique; The Discontinuity Principle; Attribute Listing; Forced Relationship Analogy; The Six Thinking Hats; Idea Smashing, etc. Most of these are variations of the two basic techniques we discussed earlier.

Planning (Involves Making Decisions)

Planning consists of three steps, each requiring us to make decisions.
1. The Vision: Predicting the future (the universe)
2. The Mission: Deciding what you want (of the future)
3. The Method: Devising ways to achieve it

When trying to predict the future, you are likely to be wrong. Therefore, you must plan for several likely scenarios. Consider these examples:

- In the 1950s they said: "When the baby-boomers and women enter the marketplace, there will be massive unemployment." (True, the labor force went up 40%; but the job market grew 50%.)

- Who said *Television* would kill the *book industry?* General Norman Schwarzkopf would not have sold thousands of copies of his book without the help of TV coverage of the Gulf war, and his personal TV appearances.

- Those who said the VCR would be the death of the movie industry were proved wrong — going to the movies is a social experience.

- In the '70s Exxon, Shell, and Texaco, all predicted crude oil at $85 per barrel (they were all wrong).

Well-trained people will be good planners. They might not stick to the plan, but they will always make good decisions.

Strategic Planning

It is fashionable to use the word *strategic* while describing even simple and straightforward "tactical" plans or investment decisions. Often consultants and managers use the word *strategic* as a buzzword; this automatically attributes greater value to the ideas they are trying to sell.

Strategic thinking aims to exploit the new and different opportunities that tomorrow will likely bring. Strategic decisions deal with issues such as technology, demographics, lifestyle, policies, geopolitics, etc., and how they affect the future direction. All these have many ramifications. *Tactical* methods try to optimize the trends of today.

Research consistently suggests that Senior Management acts as a guardian of a corporation's values and structure, rather than a seeker of maximum return on investment. Strategic planning encompasses the vision and the mission; it establishes the basic organizational purposes, objectives, and policies. Strategic planning efforts are fraught with uncertainties; therefore conformists (which means most of us) are inherently incapable of strategic thinking.

Strategic planning deals with *what* should be done, while *Tactical* planning deals with *how* it should be done. A strategic plan consists of two components:
  • A direct component that can be computed in an objective way
  • An indirect or systemic component that is likely to be subjective

The value of this second component is likely to be larger than the direct component. Also this indirect component is often influenced by extrinsic factors that generate value to the organization, which are independent of this project.

  • Mary Kay had a vision of success and independence for women (strategic); the tactic was selling cosmetics.

  • Steve Jobs (founder of Apple Computers) dreamed of integrating the world through decentralized access to information and communication (strategic); the tactic was computers.

Michael Armstrong is a master at strategic maneuvers. When he was CEO of Hughes Electronics, he saw the oncoming downturn in the defense industry, caused by thawing of relations with the Soviet Union. Recognizing the potential loss of market, he transformed Hughes from a company focused mainly on defense to a powerful competitor in the commercial electronics, space, and telecommunications industries.

When the AT&T board looked for cross-fertilization, they brought in Armstrong. He realized that the *long-distance* business (AT&T's cash-cow) was gasping for breath. He knew that the new model was going to be *"any-distance,"* powered by digital technologies. He sought strategic options and moved into new areas, which were: Local, Global, Service, Data & IP, Cable, and Wireless. This turned out to be a winner too; for the first time in 115 years, revenue from the non-voice businesses surpassed that from the voice business.

Consider another example: Say you own a company that produces engines for small equipment and you are doing quite well. However, you realize you are approaching market saturation. Without some sort of change, your business will surely plateau. Metaphorically speaking, you are fast approaching the *end of the road.* To sustain growth, you need to make some strategic decisions on which way to expand. What do you do?

You could consider expanding into foreign markets, or even consider producing mid-size engines for larger equipment.

This is exactly what happened at the Honda Motor Company. They started with small engines, moved to garden equipment, then to motorcycles, automotive engines, and cars. Now, they are on their way to building aircraft engines. It is interesting to note that even though Honda is best known for their highly reliable cars, their core business is building engines. The decision to diversify into producing vehicles came later.

Whether a particular problem falls into the strategic or tactical arena often depends on how one characterizes the problem.

If, for example, you own pipelines that transport oil, you are always looking to optimize your transport. You could add chemicals to reduce the frictional effects (resistance to motion). This is a *tactical* move, which allows you to reduce your transport cost and be more competitive. Whether you should acquire another company or look to economies of scale would be a *strategic* move.

When President Theodore Roosevelt considered strategic options to maintain his military might, he realized he had to control the seven seas. This was a *strategic* decision. Controlling the *Panama Canal* was the *tactical* option.

When dealing with "tactical" issues remember the cliché: "The devil is in the details."

- In 1891, M. Samuel & Co. (U.K.) decided to compete in the Southeast Asian market which was dominated by Standard Oil (the U.S. giant). They crafted an elaborate plan: Transport using bulk tankers; Distribute via bulk retailers, as opposed to delivering in cans; Attack all markets at the same time—to prevent price subsidies. However, this plan almost failed! Why? The assumption was that people would bring their "Standard Oil" cans to the retailers, for refilling! But they were already using these cans for many domestic needs, such as tea strainers, cups, lamp holders, spoons, toys, etc. The U.K. company did not pay attention to the *details.*

- In a more recent case, strategic planners at PepsiCo decided that it would make sense for them to diversify in the fast-food business, as this seemed a perfectly natural fit. In retaliation, McDonald's, Burger King, Wendy's, and others decided not to sell Pepsi products. This move proved disastrous for PepsiCo. Sales dropped nearly 20%. Planners at Pepsi did not pay attention to the *details.*

• A very similar error was observed at Humana. Humana started out as a hospital chain. Subsequently they decided to diversify by engaging in the HMO business. This led to a possible *perceived* conflict of interest. Other hospitals were reluctant to share information with the Humana-HMO, since that information could end up with the Humana-hospitals, a competitor. This led to the decision to separate the two groups.

———

Answers to problems in this chapter.

The Bus Stop Problem

This is a moral/ethical dilemma.
• You could pick up the old lady, deciding that because she is very ill, you should aid her first.
• Or, you could take your friend because he/she once saved your life and this would be the perfect chance to pay him/her back.
• However, you may never be able to find your perfect dream partner again.

Give the car keys to your friend and let him/her take the lady to the hospital. Stay behind and wait for the bus with the man/woman of your dreams.

If you had identified your primary objective as conquering your dream partner, the solution would have fallen into place automatically.

Eight

Time—
Invaluable and Perishable

"Dost thou love life?
Then do not squander time:
for that's the stuff life is made of."

— BENJAMIN FRANKLIN

Time, like food or airline seats, is a perishable commodity. If not utilized, its value is lost forever. Time is the most valuable commodity we have. Everyone—your friends, family, employer, volunteer organizations, etc.—vies for your time.

Research has shown consistently that in the presence of time-pressure, decision-makers tend to focus on the negative outcomes, rather than be objective.

Time is a crucial parameter in decision-making and manifests itself on three occasions.

1. As a criterion in your evaluation

- If you are trying to select a builder, time could be a criterion. Some builders might not be able to meet your timing requirements. The same might be true if you are evaluating buyers for your existing home. They may want you to move out before your other house is available.

- In war, timing is always a criterion. In Chapter 11, I discuss the Yom Kippur War, which is an excellent example of timing.

2. When you deal with candidates

When we receive information about the candidates (options), this information might already be outdated. It is always a good habit to ask:
— When was this information collected?
— Is it still valid?
— Will it be valid when we are ready to implement our action plan?

- Vista Plastics (Argentina) considered setting up a manufacturing facility in Mexico, to supply the U.S. market. They based their economic evaluations on the exchange rate applicable at the time. The project was delayed by about 18 months. During that time, the exchange rates and fiscal policies had changed and a new evaluation demonstrated that Guatemala was a better choice.

- Witlock Manufacturing was a victim of outdated information. They used geological survey maps to identify a location for a new plant in Phoenix, Arizona. Unfortunately, the maps a young engineer had downloaded were not current. When the team visited the site, they were shocked to find an apartment complex under construction.

- New technologies are highly time-sensitive, both in terms of release-to-market and obsolescence.

3. In the action phase

As stated previously, no matter how good your decision, if you do not execute it at the most propitious moment, you will not reap the maximum reward. You might even incur losses.

If we decide on a time-sensitive candidate, we need to act in a timely manner.

- Investigations revealed that Osama bin Laden's plans to blow up the U.S. embassies in Kenya and Tanzania were in the making for nearly five years. Throughout this period, he stalked his targets and waited for the right time. Even though we condemn his actions, we must admit that his timing was perfect.

- In 1989, Kodak saw the advent of the digital camera. But they did not react in a timely manner! Fourteen years after the arrival of the Sony MVC-5000, Kodak finally decided to restructure, laying off 15,000 employees (January 2004), to concentrate on *electronic imaging*. What took them so long?

- Fast-food giants such as McDonald's, Burger King, Pizza Hut, and KFC all lost a fortune, due to poor timing (see p. 153). Their decision to move to healthy foods was correct. However, they implemented their decision prematurely, i.e., before consumers were ready.

Cultural Heritage of Time

We should also recognize the influence of cultural differences in relation to time. Have you ever wondered why people from certain developing countries are not very punctual?

Fons Trompenaars[10] identified *sequential* cultures, where people think of *time* as a linear sequence of events (3:00 P.M., 4:00 P.M. . . . Monday, Tuesday . . . 1999, 2000) and *circular* cultures, where people think of time as a revolving process, like the rotation of a clock, 3:00, 6:00, 9:00, 12:00 and 3:00 again. People from circular cultures think nothing of being late for an appointment because they visualize time as a circular concept. For such cultures, time does not *run out*, it revolves. These cultures are willing to subordinate their schedules to human necessities.

Expanding Common Sense & Experience

Passage of Time and Handling Change

Imagine a couple in love. Having discussed the pros and cons of their relationship, they decide to get married. After several years, the marriage fails and they get a divorce. The perennial question is, *was it a good decision to get married to begin with?*

At first, we might be tempted to say that it was not such a good idea (decision); but we should not jump to that conclusion too rapidly. There is a good chance the couple made the best decision they could, based on the information they had at the time. Even if you make a good decision, conditions will change in unforeseeable ways with the passage of time. Success depends on how you handle change. Handling change is an integral part of decision-making. This is especially true in marriage, where values, experiences, expectations, and emotions will change over time. If a couple cannot handle the changing circumstances, their marriage will fall apart. Divorce is rarely the consequence of a bad decision to marry; more often, it is a consequence of the inability to handle change. I remind you of Darwin's comment:

> "*It is not the strongest of the species*
> *that survive, nor the most intelligent,*
> *but the one most responsive to change.*"

Nine

Selecting Criteria and Candidates

"The greatest obstacle to discovery is not ignorance; it is the illusion of knowledge. The highest form of ignorance is when you reject something you don't know anything about."

— LEE IACOCCA

Criteria Selection

Let us say you are a member of the Olympic Commitee responsible for finding the venue for the next Olympic competition.

You might consider issues related to: Safety; Local Transport; Access to International Travelers; Hotel Accommodation; Political Climate; Weather; Broadcasting Facilities; Communications; Reliability of Utilities, etc. These are criteria that impact your decision.

Likewise, if you were trying to buy a house, you would list criteria that are important to you (see box).

House Purchase Criteria

- Size of House
- Age of House
- Modern Conveniences
- Condition of House
- Front Appearance
- Floor Plan
- Number of Rooms
- Size of Garage
- Financing
- Cost per Square Foot
- Monthly Expenses
- Price of House + Repairs
- Size of Yard
- Landscaping
- Quality of Neighborhood
- Quality of Schools
- Proximity to Work
- Proximity to Buses
- Proximity to Schools
- Adverse Effects of Weather

Expanding Common Sense & Experience

All decisions are driven by a set of criteria, and a set of options/solutions. Criteria are the decision-maker's values and expectations.

Selecting appropriate criteria and assigning representative weights are vital steps in any decision-making operation.

There are two issues to consider when dealing with criteria:

1. Selecting the most relevant criteria

This is vital to making the best decision. Too often, decision-makers take a light-hearted view of this step and pay a very dear price later on. As I will show later, too many or too few criteria will compromise the decision.

2. Assigning appropriate weights to criteria

Your final decision will depend heavily on the relative values you place on your criteria. The weight assigned to each should truly represent the decision-maker's desires. When you try the examples in Part IV, you will begin to appreciate the importance of weighting criteria correctly. This topic will be discussed in detail in the next chapter.

Criteria selection is not an easy task; at times it is like groping in the dark. Even experienced professionals miss applicable criteria, only to be surprised when a competitor steals a deal. At such times you need people with diverse experience to come to your rescue. In Chapter 7, I discussed *creativity*; being creative is the only way to ensure that all relevant criteria are included in the initial analysis.

Those who invested in pharmaceutical stocks under the assumption that aging baby-boomers would create a massive demand for drugs were thoroughly disappointed. They did not look at other significant criteria:
- Prices were forced down through lobbying;
- Changes in the policies of insurance companies;

- Expiring patents;
- Decreased development of new drugs;
- Advances in gene therapy;
- A greater emphasis on prevention;
- Rapid growth of the alternative health industry.

However, there are some investment gurus who think that there is money to be made in pharmaceutical stocks, if the timing is *right*— whatever *right* means.

The power of cross-fertilization with people from different disciplines and specialties was highlighted in a crisis that faced President Bill Clinton. Told that the Mexican peso was about to collapse, he asked his advisors for an assessment of the situation. The State Department, the Federal Reserve, the Defense Department, the Immigration and Naturalization Service, U.S. Customs, the Drug Enforcement Agency, and others were instructed to come up with their assessments. Additionally, the IMF (International Monetary Fund) and the World Bank were consulted. There were many issues to consider:

- Image—a rich neighbor standing by while a poor neighbor was drowning;
- About 6 million Mexicans walking across our southern border;
- Increase of drug trafficking to support the needy;
- Overthrow of the democratic government in Mexico;
- Spread of Communism in the region through Cuban influence;
- Impact on the border patrol;
- Domino effect on other Central American countries;
- Impact on supplies to U.S. industries;
- Loan defaults;
- Compassion.

These and other criteria influenced President Clinton's decision to step in and help avert a crisis in Mexico. No one person or group would have come up with all the relevant criteria.

Consider the following problem, a true story:
A company manufacturing desalination plants wanted to hire a marketing manager to market their proprietary desalination plants in Saudi Arabia. Their human resources department (HR) identified a multitude of criteria.

They interviewed six candidates and finally selected Randy Smith, the *ideal* person. All credit to the HR folk, who felt that the position had to be filled with a male since the Arabs do not particularly like women in negotiating roles. The company made an offer, Randy accepted, quit his job, and immediately started learning the basics of the desalination trade. However, it was only when they applied for Randy's visa that they discovered he was of Jewish origin, and Saudi Arabia does not allow people of Jewish heritage to work in their country. It seems someone forgot an important prerequisite. But wait. The U.S. Equal Employment Opportunity Commission (EEOC) prohibits asking a person about his/her faith; so, even if someone had considered this possibility, there would have been a problem. Of course, there are creative ways of obtaining such information. The result was a huge expense, loss of lead-time, and loss of potential revenue. In this case timing was critical since the Saudi government was actively engaged in the expansion of their desalination facilities.

— THE MORE THE MERRIER?

A very common fallacy is that the more criteria you consider, the better the decision will be. An inexperienced coordinator is likely to include every conceivable criterion in the evaluation process. Our studies of the selection processes for *dating services, real estate, employee recruiting,* and *bid evaluations* demonstrated convincingly that using a large number of criteria is counter-productive, as it tends to dilute the significance of each criterion.

In our studies, we used an advanced *algorithmic* technique to identify the impact of the number of criteria and found that the optimum number of criteria is between eight and twelve. Beyond this range, additional criteria often

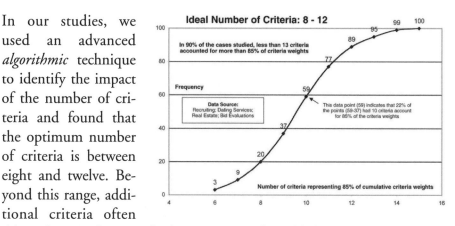

dilute the significance of other criteria and are likely to yield a suboptimal decision.

Consider a simple example:

> Imagine that you are buying a house and you have decided on ten criteria. You simply assign equal weights to each of them (10% to each). Your wife then looks at the list and adds five more criteria. Now, you have to redistribute your weights, and assuming again that you weighted them equally, this time each criterion would have 6.67%. Your criteria no longer have the same significance as they originally had; their importance has been diluted. Does this accurately represent your preferences?

The best approach to criteria selection is to start with as many as you can think of, and then use an algorithmic technique, such as *XpertUS*, to determine the most relevant ones.

Beware of overbearing executives who think they are the only ones who are capable of creative ideas. They are quick to say, "*How can Joe come up with a solution? He knows nothing about our system.*" In fact, this might be the exact reason why Joe can see the creative solution. Everyone else is too close to the problem. Also recognize that creativity is expressed in many different ways, and everyone has the capacity to be creative. Beware of pessimists who think nothing new will work—*we need to stick to what we know*, is their motto.

A few years ago, New Zealand's economy was threatened by a large market swing from butter to margarine. The dairy industry is the mainstay of New Zealand's economy; hence any slowdown in sales would be catastrophic. Although management thought they knew the reasons, they hired a market research consultant to find out what enticed housewives to switch. To their surprise, the principal reason given was *ease of spreading*. They now had an important criterion that they had not thought of, and were ready to move on to managing the decision-making phase.

Recall our discussion on the power of creative thinking when identifying options? It applies equally to the selection of criteria.

— SECONDARY OBJECTIVES
Sometimes there are multiple objectives or secondary objectives. On the Middle East problem, President George W. Bush has to appear to be impartial, but he also has to appease the Republican voters. A Gallup poll indicated that 66% of the Republican voters were sympathetic to the Israelis, while only 8% supported the Palestinians. Naturally, Republican politicians would demand that *voter-acceptance* be one of the criteria in any evaluation. Now the President has a *secondary* objective. This becomes a criterion which has nothing to with the Middle East crisis, but has everything to do with the Republicans staying in power. Thus, when searching for criteria, make sure you have a very clear vision of your objectives.

—⫘⫘—

Additionally, it is important to be consistent in the way you define your criteria. Always try to state your criteria in positive terms. Consider two criteria when purchasing a car—*purchase price* and *hours between overhauls.* While a "low price" is attractive, "low hours between overhauls" is undesirable because it means more maintenance. This could lead to confusion.

Also try to be specific—i.e., *room temperature* does not tell you what temperature is desirable; a *room temperature of no more than 75°* is more meaningful.

In the next chapter, I will discuss how to use criteria in the decision-making process.

Candidate Selection

Candidates are the possible solutions to a problem—the options. The basic requirements for identifying candidates are presented below.

— CREATIVITY

In Chapter 7, I discussed creativity in detail. Creative thinking is vital to generate a good list of candidates or options. No matter how good your decision-making tool, if you do not have a good list of candidates, you will not arrive at a good decision.

It is easy to reject an idea or a candidate, but it is extremely difficult to generate one to start with. Having a reasonable selection of candidates is highly desirable, but when there are too many choices, the decision-making process becomes confusing.

In the country of Sri Lanka, in the 2001 elections, there were over 5000 candidates representing seventeen political parties running for 225 seats—i.e., about 22 candidates per seat. Would you consider this to be excessive for a country one-tenth the size of the state of Texas, with a population of about 18 million?

— "Perishability"

During candidate selection, it is important to ask the question—*are the candidates perishable?*

When we refer to perishable goods, we usually think of food; yet, there are many other perishable items. Consider airline seats. If not sold prior to take-off, they are considered to have *perished.* The same is true of restaurant chairs, cinema seats, and even your barber's chair. If not utilized, their value at a given moment is gone—in essence, they perish without generating any revenue.

Recently, I traveled from Houston to Mexico City on a business trip. Because of business obligations, I bought a fully-refundable ticket, paying $525.00. On the day before departure, my wife decided to join me on the flight. She sat next to me, having paid just $242.00. After waiting as long as possible, airlines liquidate any remaining tickets. It is better to get something for the empty seats rather than let them perish.

This theory has made its way to other *perishable* products. Delivery capacity on gas transportation systems is also perishable; hence, it is traded like airline seats. *Firm* capacity, guaranteeing delivery, is sold at a higher price. Any unused capacity is sold at a lower rate as *alternate-firm* and *interruptible* capacity; if the excess capacity is not sold on a given day, it is lost. The same is true of telephone lines, electrical power lines, etc.; if not utilized, their value at that instant is lost.

Thus, when we consider candidates (possible solutions to a problem), we need to consider their *perishable* nature.

— Prerequisites

Once we have a list of candidates, we need to subject them to the test of *prerequisites*. A candidate that does not meet *prerequisites* should be rejected. Even experienced evaluators fail to recognize the significance of *prerequisites* (minimum conditions that must be satisfied), which are pre-qualifying factors.

Prerequisites have two possible origins.

1. Specified *a priori.* This elicits a simple *Yes* or *No* response.

   • Consider the minimum vehicle emission requirements for automobiles, set by the federal government. Any used car dealer considering importing vehicles to the U.S. would set this as a *prerequisite.* Candidate vehicles under consideration either do or do not meet the *prerequisites.*

   • Imagine you are looking for a project manager for a client in Saudi Arabia. The client specifies that the person should be *non-Jewish*; this is a *prerequisite* specified *a priori.* The client might even insist that the person is a *male* and a *Moslem.*

2. A *limiting condition* of a criterion.

   • A homebuyer has an upper limit on his/her monthly payments. Thus, while monthly payment is an *evaluation* criterion, it also imposes a *prerequisite.*

These *in* or *out* guidelines must be well defined and handled with care. If overly stringent *prerequisites* are specified, you might eliminate a perfectly acceptable candidate. However, you do not require an elaborate method for this process of elimination. A simple table will suffice.

While criteria associated with *prerequisites* are not included in the evaluation, criteria associated with *limiting conditions* must be included in the evaluation.

Sometimes the decision-maker is not concerned with candidate selection, as in beauty contests and in horse races, where the candidates have been pre-selected. However, the decision-maker still has to gather information on the candidates and rank them.

— Assumptions

When you have to make a decision you start with some assumptions. These translate into criteria, which in turn are the prerequisites, limiting conditions, etc. Often, it is advisable to see how sensitive your decision is to a particular assumption.

For many years, battles against terrorists and assassins were based on the assumption that the perpetrators would want to preserve their own lives. However, with the advent of the cult of *suicide-bombers,* law enforcement agencies have been forced to review all their security measures and procedures. Likewise, airline security systems have been thrown into disarray.

Always challenge your assumptions!

Ten

The Ranking Process

"We all have possibilities we don't know about.
We can do things we don't even dream we can do."

— DALE CARNEGIE

In the previous chapter, I said that assigning weights to criteria was vital. However, first we must segregate criteria.

Criteria Segregation

The criteria you identify fall into three groups:
1. Prerequisites (*for candidate selection*)
2. Obligatory Criteria (*need-to-have evaluation criteria*)
3. Desirables (*nice-to-have features*)

Even though prerequisites are used to select candidates, they themselves are criteria.

This is best explained using a case study. An airline company recently issued a tender for catering services in Chicago.

If the airline wanted the supplier to be located in Chicago, *location* would be a *prerequisite*—bidders (service provider) located in other areas would be eliminated.

If the location of the service provider is immaterial, but being in Chicago would be an added convenience—this would be a *desirable* feature. If, however, communication needs and transport issues during inclement weather are of concern, then the *location* of the service provider should be an *obligatory* criterion.

Prerequisites and *desirables* should not be considered in the ranking process.

Studies have shown that most people tend to assume all criteria are of equal value, and then start shifting their values from one moment to the next. A disciplined approach will serve you well. I now provide a proven technique to segregate and identify the most relevant criteria.

Start by selecting an adequate number of criteria, but try not to exceed twenty. Now, look at all the criteria and identify and remove prerequisites. Even though prerequisites apply only to candidate selection, they must be defined during the criteria-selection phase.

Whittle down these criteria to a reasonable number (around 12) that represent your main wants and needs; these are the *obligatory* criteria. This can be done using one of two methods.

1. Your subjective judgment—(dangerous) or
2. The pairwise comparison technique (e.g. *XpertUS*, discussed in Chapter 11).

The rejected criteria are the *desirables*; these should not be included in the evaluation.

Now that you have the *obligatory* criteria, it is time to assign weights to represent your desires. In all my work, I have seen additional criteria surface during the information-gathering phase. As you think more about a problem and start gathering information, you will often detect other relevant criteria. Add these new criteria to your original list and repeat the *criteria segregation process.*

Criteria Weighting

Sadly, there are many books and software products on decision-making that consider all criteria to be of the same significance or importance. This is not so in the real world. If you ask a homebuyer to rate *the need to be close to work* vs. *the need to live in a safe neighborhood,* they would probably not be of equal importance.

Presently, evaluators use one of two common methods to assign criteria weights.

1. The *distribution* technique:
   Where 100% is distributed among the criteria.

2. The *scaling* technique:
   Where each criterion is assigned a number on a scale of 1–10. (1 = low preference). Normalize the assigned values (add all the numbers, divide each by the total, then multiply by 100). Often a scale of 1–5 is used. Sometimes qualitative words such as *excellent, good,* etc., are used to represent preferences.

Try the example below and see the difference between the weighting techniques. This simple example also demonstrates how fallible we humans are at making decisions.

EXAMPLE: **Allocating spare time** (use the table shown below)
Imagine you have 100 hours of spare time per month and would like to spend them on the activities shown in the table below.

First, distribute the hours among these activities (*distribution* technique). Repeat the exercise, this time assigning weights using the *scaling* technique. Compare the two results.

If you were faced with a real decision, which one would you use? Until recently we have had to rely on *common sense and experience* to assign weights. Return to this problem after you have read the next chapter and compare these rankings against weightings obtained using *XpertUS*.

How would you distribute 100 hours among these activities?

Activity	Distribution %	Scaling (1-10)	Scaling %	XpertUS* %
1. Spiritual Activities				
2. Education/Training				
3. Physical Fitness				
4. Family Life				
5. Charity & Volunteer Work				
6. Hobbies & Pleasure Activities				
7. Income Producing Work				
Total >>>	100%		100%	100%

* You can fill in the *XpertUS* column only after you read Chapter 11.

Candidate Ranking

In any decision-making scenario, there is almost always a trade-off. Whether you are investing money, buying a home, or making almost any decision, it is imperative that you are cognizant of the consequences and trade-offs before you start the ranking process. In addition to the pros and cons of each candidate, there are other issues associated with uncertainty of information and the individual's tolerance for risk.

Opportunity thrives in the realm of uncertainty. The examples shown below carry a certain degree of uncertainty, yet we have to make decisions based on our best judgment.

- Based on past performance, house prices in the city you plan to move to (to retire) will appreciate at 7% per annum. Should you buy now?

- As computers become more accessible, more kids will follow computer-related courses, and there could be a surplus of computer science graduates. Should your son study computer science?

- It is highly probable that the government will privatize the Social Security system; hence the stock market will soar to unprecedented levels. Should you load up on stocks?

All of us have to decide how much risk we are willing to take. When you make a decision, you must factor in your tolerance to risk.

- When you purchase insurance, you decide on the deductible, based on how averse you are to risk and losses.

- Should you continue to be an employee or should you start your own business?

- In 2001, the average equity mutual fund (stocks only) provided an annualized average return of 10.38%. The risk, as measured by a volatility index, was a standard deviation of 21.61. For a balanced mutual fund (a mix of bonds and stocks), the return over the same period was 8.80%, with a volatility index of only 10.28. You have to decide which one is suitable for you.

If you are mathematically inclined, you will note that balanced funds offered 85% of the return provided by the equity stock funds, but with only half the risk.

These are risky ventures; the risk-to-reward ratio is inherent in our economy. Such decisions are unique to each individual. In Part II of this book I discuss how to manage these types of decisions.

⸺

Now we are ready to assign weights to the criteria and rank the candidates. I propose you use one of two methods:

1. The *Matrix* Method (see below)

2. *XpertUS* (highly recommended; explained in Chapter 11)

The Matrix Method

The matrix method is the most common technique used by businesses for making decisions. It is designed to rank the candidates being considered, be they employees, consultants, schools, products, or anything else. The process is as follows:

1. Identify all relevant criteria;
2. Assign weights to these criteria to represent their relative importance using common sense;
3. Select an acceptable group of candidates;
4. For each criterion, compare all candidates and assign points to represent their significance;

5. Finally, multiply the points by the weights to determine the rankings.

EXAMPLE

I was a member of the evaluation team for a multimillion-dollar oil refinery project for which competitive bids were requested. The evaluation criteria were determined to be: *experience, personnel, latest technology, financial,* and *schedule* (each had sub-criteria). Weights were assigned based on *common sense and experience.*

Each candidate was then assigned a perceived weight with respect to each of the five criteria.

The bids indicated the following:
- Bidder A had extensive *experience* in project management and construction.
- Bidder B (French) had the best *personnel* and the latest *technology.*
- Bidder C had the best *price* and *financing.*

A background survey indicated:
- The CFO (Chief Financial Officer) had connections to Bidder A. He was trained by them and later worked for them as a consultant.
- The wife of the CEO was French and had connections to Bidder B. She and her husband had plans to retire and move to France.
- The host country was receiving financial aid from the country of Bidder C. Several local politicians and the mayor of the town in which the refinery was to be located were partial to Bidder C.

Each person or faction pushed to weight criteria in favor of his/her preferred party. For example, the CFO argued that *experience* needed to carry 40% of the weight. The CEO insisted that *technology* and *per-*

Weaknesses of the Matrix Method

1. Criteria Selection: Were all relevant criteria selected? There is no way to control unconscious subjectivity while determining criteria (remember the examples I presented in Chapter 1, under Human Element).

2. Criteria Weighting: Did we err or express bias in the assignment of weights? Relying on personal judgment to determine weights is extremely difficult and risky. Assigning weights can also be skewed by vested interests.

3. Group Comparison: It is almost impossible to evaluate five or six candidates as a group with regard to multiple criteria and accurately determine relative superiority.

sonnel should account for at least 50% of the weight. And of course, friends of Bidder C pushed for 40% for *pricing/finance.* This was a decision-maker's worst nightmare.

Although the matrix method has many disadvantages (see box), this was the only option for us.

To the reader, I recommend the *XpertUS* technique discussed in the next chapter. Do not skip ahead; continue reading sequentially, as it provides a better foundation for understanding and utilizing the technique presented later on.

Other Methods

Here are a few other methods that have been proposed, though they are rarely used in any serious decision-making situations.

— THE PROS & CONS METHOD (PCM)

As the name suggests, this involves simply listing the benefits and the negatives, then making a rational decision.

— The PMI Technique

PMI stands for "Plus/Minus/Implications." Although highly subjective, it is a remarkable improvement on the PCM technique.

— Force Field Analysis

Force field analysis is a useful technique for looking at all the forces for and against a decision. In effect, it is a specialized version of the PCM method. By carrying out the analysis, you can plan to strengthen the forces supporting a decision and reduce the impact of opposition to it.

I urge you not to use these methods. The *XpertUS* technique is far superior to any other, and easier to use.

What Next!

You have completed your ranking evaluation and have before you a list of candidates ranked in order of preference. T.S. Eliot once said: *Between the idea and the action, there is a shadow.*

Do not let your emotions get the better of you. When you selected the candidates, you passed them through an evaluation process to ensure they met all the *prerequisites.* This means they were all acceptable candidates. Do not reject the top-ranked candidate simply because of a preconceived notion. It is surprising how frequently people try to do this. They have a preconceived notion of who or what should be selected and, when the process of evaluation selects a different candidate, they do not accept it even though it is their own evaluation criteria and judgment that led to the selection of this candidate.

Peter Drucker once had an assignment from Alfred P. Sloan, the Chairman and CEO of General Motors. Sloan said to Drucker, "Say what you have to say and do not worry about how we would react. Don't concern yourself with compromises that would make your recommendations acceptable. Every executive here can make compromises, but they cannot make the right compromise, *unless you tell them what (you believe) is right."*

If the rankings are very close, you can then look at the *desirables.* You could even rank the candidates using *XpertUS*, considering the *desirables* as criteria; but generally a cursory look at the other benefits will allow you to arrive at a meaningful decision.

Sufficiency vs. Optimality

My work in the decision-making arena revealed the issue of *sufficiency* to be that which creates the greatest confusion for most people. All ranking methods rank candidates in order of superiority/preference, tending to the *optimal.* However, the optimal candidate might be outside the limits of the decision-maker. We can use a *Curve of Diminishing Returns* (CDR) to meet our requirements.

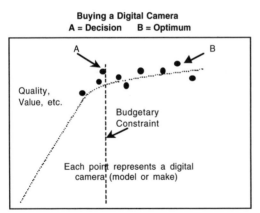

Buying a Digital Camera
A = Decision   B = Optimum

A

B

Quality, Value, etc.

Budgetary Constraint

Each point represents a digital camera (model or make)

Cost, Effort, Energy, etc.

I used this method recently to buy a digital camera. I started by gathering information on criteria such as: Price; Pixels; Optical Zoom; Name Brand; Movie option; Video playback; Battery life; Cost of accessories; Viewfinder; Memory. Then I used *XpertUS* to rank (*value*) the various cameras. I did not use *price* as a criterion in the evaluation. The CDR graph of *value* against *price*, is shown here. I finally decided to purchase the camera represented by point "A".

In fact, this type of curve applies to almost any item you purchase, and to most tasks you undertake.

Other examples might be:

- Adding upgrades to your new home. A similar graph would show the *benefit/improvement* increases with *effort.* You could look at it as an increase in value for every additional dollar spent. The first $20,000 you spend would increase the value of the home by $12,000, but the next $20,000 might only increase the value by another $8,000.

- A baseball coach trying to decide on signing a pitcher. He might be trying to decide if he should pay top-dollar for the best player or settle for *value for money.*

- A company building a refinery; how much redundancy there should be.

- If you are selecting a university, you might have *academic limitations;* thus deciding on the optimum university might not be advisable. True, if you had used *academic limitations* as a criterion, this would be reflected in your optimum selection. In this case, *academic limitations* would be the equivalent of *cost.*

In all these cases you have to decide when *quality* would be sufficient; any additional money or effort would only produce a marginal benefit.

It is important to note that if you do not have any constraints or limitations, you do not need to plot a CDR; in such a case you would, of course, use *price* as a criterion in your evaluation. Similarly, if you make *price* a limiting prerequisite, you do not need a CDR.

Eleven

XpertUS and the Pairwise Technique

*"You must learn from the mistakes of others.
You can't possibly live long enough
to make them all yourself."*

— SAM LEVENSON

For years, literature on decision-making has touted the need for clear thinking, logic, reasoning, maturity, common sense, experience, wisdom, rational judgment, etc.; but if we follow these suggestions, decision-making is reserved for an elite few.

Today's manager is bombarded with an enormous amount of data generated by IT departments. All this overpowers traditional decision-making methods. Managers need a simple tool that does not require a huge investment of time or money. How can the average person make winning decisions? Something new is needed.

What caused the stock price to drop:

- Competitive emerging technology from a rival company;

- Management problems—such as the departure of the CEO/CFO;

- Negative news governing accounting practices;

- The merger of two other competitors;

- New regulatory issues;

- Impact of geopolitics;

- The industry group as a whole dropped due to inherent problems;

- The market as a whole dropped due to federal policy, recession, etc.

Most stockbrokers use highly sophisticated mathematical tools to select stocks. They set a target buy-price for a stock. When the stock reaches this price they receive a buy-signal; yet they do not act on this signal alone. They make some value judgments (see box—p. 121). These are qualitative issues that require human intervention.

Remember, if you rely purely on *common sense and experience*, you are going to be a victim of subjectivity and human limitations, as was confirmed by Dr. Miller. You need a decision-making tool that is able to process qualitative judgments, yet allows you to make the final determination.

Earlier in this book I referred to the *XpertUS* software, but I did not elaborate. This was to let you first understand the basics of decision-making.

XpertUS is a decision-making tool, which allows you to navigate through your feelings, desires, and expectations to arrive at a well-thought-out decision. *XpertUS* does not make the decision; it is the vehicle that leads you through the process. *You* make the decision! *You* are always in control. You simply tell *XpertUS* how you feel about criteria and candidates.

The *XpertUS* software applies sophisticated mathematical techniques to the process of ranking (criteria and/or candidates), thus allowing for objective and scientific analyses. The *XpertUS* software also incorporates random-sampling techniques to validate both the process and the outcome.

XpertUS is designed to handle both quantitative and qualitative criteria. (The cost of a car is *quantitative*, while the comfort of the ride is *qualitative*.) Similarly, *XpertUS* can handle *obligatory* and *desirable* criteria. For example, when building a house, it is *obligatory* to remain within a given budget, yet it might be *desirable* to make the bedrooms smaller in order to add a study.

The *XpertUS* Process

The *XpertUS Decision-Maker* is a three-step decision-making tool, within the seven-step process, that helps make optimum decisions by minimizing subjectivity and ensuring transparency.

1. *Describe* the problem in as much detail as possible. Experts agree that a proper definition of the problem provides fifty percent of the solution.

2. *Dissect* the problem by breaking it down and identifying relevant criteria. Many decision-makers commit the error of eliminating criteria or candidates based entirely on personal experience or bias. Use *XpertUS* to determine which criteria are important (assign weights).

3. *Decide* using pairwise comparisons to determine the relative superiority of candidates for each criterion (see discussion below). *XpertUS* does not require the decision-maker to look at all the candidates at the same time and assign points. The pairwise comparison technique used by *XpertUS* is reliable because most people can easily compare two items and express their thoughts and feelings about the relative merits of one over the other.

For example, using the multimillion-dollar oil refinery example from Chapter 10, one may think *technology* is the most important criterion. With *XpertUS*, it is easy to determine how important *technology* is when compared to the other criteria. Indeed, determining the degree of importance for each criterion is a vital step in decision-making.

Utilizing powerful mathematics, *XpertUS* processes this pairwise information to assign weights to each criterion and points to each candidate. Finally, *XpertUS* provides a ranked decision supported by a *reliability index.* This index tells how consistent the evaluation is and whether the results are reliable.

The *XpertUS Decision-Maker* does not take the decision-making process away from humans. Rather, it is a high-powered tool to organize, analyze, rank, and validate the criteria and candidates (options) in a given decision-making situation.

Pairwise Comparison Vs. Group Comparison

Under the *matrix* method (Chapter 10), I discussed the two popular methods of assigning weights to criteria. These were the *distribution* method and the *scaling* method. I noted that the two methods almost always gave different weightings. There is no way to decide which one is correct. Furthermore, as I indicated earlier, the matrix method is seriously flawed.

Now let us consider another method, the *pairwise* comparison technique. This is the method used in the *XpertUS* program.

In normal ranking studies, the evaluator looks at the information pertaining to each candidate, compares them as a group, and assigns relative points. In the pairwise technique, the evaluator looks at any pair of candidates and indicates how superior one candidate is when compared with the other. This comparison is repeated for all the combinations of candidates. The same technique is used to assign weights to criteria—comparing a pair of criteria each time.

Imagine you are a judge in a beauty contest. This is a situation with many criteria, such as *facial beauty, physical attributes, personality, education, talents, appearance in different attire, etc.* You are required to compare a group of contestants, weight them for each criterion, and arrive at a ranking. If you were to repeat this exercise three months later, you would almost certainly arrive at a different ranking.

This is to be expected because we are human, and prone to subjectivity. However, with *XpertUS* you would be conducting pairwise comparisons. This guarantees a minimal degree of subjectivity.

The pairwise technique is best illustrated by considering just one criterion. Imagine you are seated in an airport lounge. The faces of two beautiful ladies appear on a TV screen. I ask you to distribute 100 points between these two, reflecting your concept of beauty. You might say, 40-60, 50-50, 70-30, and so on. This is your choice. A few minutes later, the TV screen displays four pictures of ladies. Once again, I ask you to distribute 100 points among the four ladies. You do this again; probably it took you a little longer. A few minutes later, seven pictures are displayed and you distribute 100 points among these ladies as well.

You would agree that as the number of candidates increased, it became increasingly difficult to make a reliable judgment.

This short mental exercise confirms that *comparing a pair* requires less effort than comparing a group, and is certainly far more reliable and consistent.

Tests conducted by the author have proven this to be the case. See Appendix 4 for a more complete discussion on the reliability of *XpertUS*.

Powerful Features of *XpertUS*

— SENSITIVITY STUDIES

- Imagine you are planning to buy a home and *distance-to-work* is a criterion in your decision-making. You go through the entire process of evaluation using *XpertUS* to obtain a ranking of homes. After further consideration, you feel that you could find a job closer to home if need be. The "What-If" mode of *XpertUS* is ideal for sensitivity studies. You do not have to conduct the candidate evaluation all over again; *XpertUS* retains your original evaluation data and uses it in the sensitivity analysis.

- Imagine another scenario. A purchasing manager considering buying automobiles for the fleet might assign a 30% weight to *reliability*. It turns out that all the candidates are highly reliable, and there is not much that separates them. We realize that this heavy weight assigned to *reliability* dwarfs the impact of the other criteria. We call this a *top-skewed* scenario; so we make *reliability* of a certain minimum level a prerequisite, and remove it from the evaluation.

You may think that structured decision-making is a lot of work, but you need to consider the cost of a poor decision.

— Consolidating Decisions

In many situations, more than one person is involved in the decision-making process; thus we need a method to arrive at a consensus.

In Chapter 13, I discuss working with others and the various techniques available to consolidate decisions made by a group. *XpertUS* provides all these techniques in the *Consolidator* mode.

— Performance Evaluation (Peer Evaluation)

Individuals within a team can evaluate the team using XpertUS. Then the team-leader can consolidate the individual decisions, to arrive at composite ranking. The final rankings provided by this technique have been used to distribute bonuses, award grades, promote candidates, etc.

Twelve

Implementing Your Decision

"Ideas are worthless. Intentions have no power.
Plans are nothing ... unless they are followed with action."
— GENERAL DOUGLAS MACARTHUR

No book on decision-making is complete without a discussion on the *implementation* of your decision.

Why are most Americans overweight? Have we not been told over and over of the need to keep our weight under control? An overweight person is prone to high blood pressure, cardiac problems, problems with joints, etc. Yes, we have all been well-schooled on the problems of obesity. Likewise, at one time or another, all of us have made attempts to get our weight under control. Yet many of us fail. We do well at taking care of our vehicles and other possessions, but neglect our health. The problem is not in the decision-making, but in the *execution* of the decision!

We have discussed extensively the techniques of making the optimum decision. Now that you have made your final decision, do not second-guess it. It is your decision and you need to develop faith in it and be in harmony with it.

You may have seen a nature program about a cheetah on the hunt. What is the cheetah's strategy? He surveys the terrain and picks his target (*decides*); he then moves stealthily into the area, crouches, and waits for the most opportune moment (*times*); then, suddenly, he leaps out (*executes*). He knows that to stay alive he must follow through with this process day after day. The *success triangle* is built around the same process—it has three components:

1. *Deciding* on the correct path or action;
2. *Timing* the execution (patience is a virtue);
3. *Executing* it with tenacious persistence.

3. Execute

I intentionally spent a considerable amount of time on the first element of the *success* triangle. If you reach a sub-optimal decision, it would require an inordinate amount of extra effort to generate the desired result.

It is now time to look at the other two facets of the *success* triangle.

Timing

Think for a moment how natural and important timing is. If you decide to approach your supervisor for a favor, you would intuitively wait for a moment when he/she is not under pressure, when he/she is in a good mood. Yet, when it comes to implementing our well-thought-out decision, we completely forget how critical *timing* is. We become emotionally attached to our decision and try to execute it immediately.

When soldiers are deployed on enemy beaches, military strategists seek the best approach, paying attention to the geography and the terrain. Then they might wait till nightfall, avoiding a full moon and seeking the appropriate tide before they move. That is *timing*.

One of the best examples of excellent *timing* is what is known today as the Yom Kippur War.

On October 6, 1973 (on *Yom Kippur*, the holiest day for the Jewish people), Syria and Egypt attacked Israel from the Golan Heights and across the Suez Canal respectively, surprising Israel and outnumbering them 12 to 1.

It is important to be aware that what is urgent might not necessarily be that which is important. Often, how an idea is conceived makes the difference between the *urgent* and the *important.* Urgency is time-related, and requires immediate action. Importance is driven by values. If ignored, important items could turn into urgent items.

When considering timing, do not forget the perishable nature of the information used to arrive at the decision. Sometimes the candidates can become obsolete by the time you are ready to execute your decision. *XpertUS* is well suited for determining the ideal time to execute your plan.

Note that *not doing anything* is also an option. Quite often, decision-makers exclude this option from consideration simply because it is difficult to identify the *pros* and *cons* of not doing anything.

Next is the final leg of the *success* triangle.

Execution

The path between today's dream and tomorrow's reality is often long and arduous.

Is it necessary to be persistent to be successful? The answer is an emphatic yes. Without persistence you are less likely to achieve your goals and objectives. You may encounter moments of difficulty and frustration, but do not despair; they are only temporary. If you want to succeed, you need to proceed with tenacious persistence.

Consider these examples:

- In 1970, Xerox Corporation put together a team of world-class researchers charged with creating *the architecture of informa-tion*,[11] a groundbreaking concept. Scientists at the Xerox Palo Alto Research Center (PARC) lived up to the challenge by inventing distributed computing, graphical user interfaces, the first commercial mouse, bit-mapped displays, Ethernet, client/server architecture, object-oriented programming, laser printing, and many of the basic protocols of the Internet. They were a persistent bunch.

- John Saxon, a fighter pilot, decided to teach algebra at a junior college. Soon he realized the techniques being used were inade-quate. He developed an entirely new method of teaching, based on student participation. His technique was a huge success; yet, when he tried to publish a book, none of the publishers were interested. Driven by his conviction, and with tenacious persis-tence, he decided to self-publish. Today, he has sold in excess of two million copies.

- Federal Express (FedEx) would not be around today if not for Fred Smith's tenacious persistence. While a student at Yale, he came up with the idea for Federal Express. The postmaster gen-eral, UPS, his business professors, and his friends said that no one would pay a fancy price for speed and reliability—the rest is history.

- The saving of Chrysler Corporation from bankruptcy is a classic illustration of the tenacious persistence of a group of people (see box).

The Story of Chrysler

When Chrysler was facing bankruptcy, they started looking for options to solve their problem. They recognized that timing was vital. They were creative and persistent. The board was committed to turning Chrysler around. The rescue plan was implemented with the aid of many parties. Singly none could have done anything for Chrysler; but together, they worked it out. Literally, society came to Chrysler's rescue.

The U.S. government granted $1.5 billion in federal loan guarantees and Canada gave $200 million more. State and local governments came up with $357 million. Banks provided the company with $642 million in new loans, with deferred interest, or interest give-ups. Suppliers and dealers granted $63 million in concessions, and the United Auto Workers Union agreed to a three-year labor contract that would save Chrysler $462 million in wages and benefits.

- President John F. Kennedy had a fervent belief when he made the commitment to landing a man on the moon.

- JVC persisted for twenty years (1957-1977) before the successful release of the VCR.

Remember, nothing in life is free, not even the air you breathe. Whatever you do or want has a price. This is not necessarily money—it can be time, energy, emotions, health, stress, or peace of mind—but there is always a price.

A famous quote from Franklin P. Jones reminds us that, *when you get something for nothing, you just haven't been billed for it yet.*

A very noteworthy example of tenacious persistence is documented in the movie *Cool Runnings*. If you have not seen this movie, I recommend it very highly.

Cool Runnings is the true story of the Jamaican bobsledding team that participated in the 1988 Winter Olympics in Canada. Jamaica is a tropical island without snow. Jamaica and Winter Olympics might sound preposterous. How on earth would Jamaica have bobsledding athletes, let alone athletes worthy of the Winter Olympics? The Jamaican team persisted, even when all the experts were saying that this was an impossible dream. Watch the movie for the rest of the story.

Of course, history is littered with stories of those who regretted not having pursued a dream. Here is one example.

Phillip Reiss had invented a machine that would transmit music. He was days away from inventing *the telephone*. Yet, everybody around him said that there would never be a need for a telephone. Fifteen years later, Alexander Graham Bell invented the telephone and made millions.

A favorite saying I formed:

> *Have a clear vision and develop a fervent belief,*
> *then pursue it with singularity of purpose,*
> *and tenacious persistence.*

Thirteen

Working With Others

> *"How can one conceive of a one-party system
> in a country that has over
> two hundred varieties of cheese?"*
>
> — CHARLES DE GAULLE

Delegating Decision-Making

Management pays lip service to *delegation,* hailing it as a catalyst to efficiency; yet, how many of us actually practise this approach?

Decision-making has to be delegated at all levels of management, but many managers work long hours trying to understand every detail about everything. They want to make every decision. They think that if they don't make all the decisions, operations will grind to a halt. The rationalized justification is that subordinates do not possess the experience necessary to make these decisions.

Managers think that *Joe* does not possess the experience, common sense, wisdom, logic, reasoning, gut-feelings, judgment, maturity, ability to think clearly, or analytical skills to be trusted with decision-making. In his best-selling book, *The One Minute Manager,*[12] Ken Blanchard stresses the virtues of delegation.

It would, however, be foolish to delegate before providing subordinates with the necessary tools and training to make optimum decisions. This book will enhance their understanding of decision-making, and *XpertUS* is an ideal training tool.

Ask *Joe* to test his decision using *XpertUS*, then ask him to present the conclusions with and without the use of *XpertUS*. You, as the supervisor, will then have that extra degree of confidence that *Joe* did think through the process. You have nothing to lose and everything to gain!

Team Decisions and Peer Evaluations

Whether it is the U.S. Congress or the board of a large corporation, most crucial decisions are made within groups or teams. Often the group consists of representatives (specialists) for each of the evaluation criteria. Where necessary, each specialist on the team can form his/her own sub-group. While groups can provide a range of specialized know-how, history has shown that groups are often ineffective at coming to optimum decisions. Yale University psychologist Irving Janis called this phenomenon *groupthink:* a deterioration of mental effectiveness, practical considerations, and moral judgment as a result of various group process factors.

Those of us who are old enough remember the horror of the *Challenger* disaster. On January 28, 1986, people all over the planet were watching the takeoff of *Challenger*, a manned NASA space shuttle. Just over a minute into the flight, the spacecraft exploded and burst into flames. The world was in shock. How could an eminent organization such as NASA have failed so catastrophically?

Following several high-level enquiries, a panel of experts concluded the fundamental cause was an engineering flaw. The rocket seals had failed under freezing temperatures. Prior to the launch, engineers had reason to believe there were potential seal problems. They had cautioned NASA against the launch until they had time to study this further. NASA made a bad decision. Were they a victim of *groupthink?*

In fact, a panel concluded that in the more recent *Columbia* disaster, various committees had granted over 1600 safety waivers! *Groupthink?*

Harvey Pitt resigned as Chairman of the Securities and Exchange Commission, after just 15 months in the job, among a myriad of allegations. Earlier, the Senate had unanimously confirmed Pitt, hailing him as a savior. This is another example of the dangers of groupthink.

Consider the controversial subject of the death penalty. Different nations have made different decisions on this; not just in terms of what crimes and circumstances deserve the penalty of death, but even on the sheer merit of the death penalty itself. Why? It comes down to values and emotions. Sometimes when we cannot agree on something, we simply subjugate our beliefs for the comfort of a consensus.

Being part of a team adds a new dimension to our decision-making efforts. If you observe the dynamics of group interaction, you will observe that members of the group fall into one of three categories.

1. There will be a couple of natural leaders who are very vocal; they set the tone and tenor of the discussion.

2. A few provide occasional input, but are often forced into oblivion by the vocal few.

3. Most try to maintain harmony or tend to stay in a comfort zone of no conflict. They contribute nothing to the event and basically go along with the crowd.

It has been said that if Thomas Edison had worked with a focus group, he would have developed a very large candle instead of the light bulb.

I fully advocate team decision-making. It helps bring out the best in each of us and, because it offers cross-fertilization of ideas, has the potential to produce the optimum solution. However, the process must be managed to allow for universal participation.

Sadly, most teams would simply take the average of the group's decision and arrive at a consensus, without any attention to the varying levels of expertise of the team members or the process used in the evaluation. This degrades the quality of the evaluation. What is needed is a consolidation technique that recognizes the various levels of expertise.

Beware, Group Cognitive processes can sometimes lead to a *whole* that is less valuable than its *parts*.

Consolidation Techniques

Consolidating multiple decisions is serious business; do not underestimate its value. How one consolidates an evaluation to arrive at the final ranking depends on the manner in which individual evaluations are conducted. Let us consider the two main consolidation techniques.

A. CRITERIA-CONSOLIDATION

Each *group* leader is a member of the evaluation team. Here each *group* would conduct an independent evaluation, and rank the bidders considering *only* its specialty criterion. Typically one would use a comparative technique such as *XpertUS*. The objective is to consolidate the rankings obtained by the candidates for the various criteria. Thus we need to conduct a *criteria-consolidation*.

This technique is perhaps best seen in terms of a project on which I was a consultant.

A Texas utility company invited bids from engineering companies to build and operate three pump stations.

Table A. Criteria-Consolidation					
Bidders > >		**Simco**	**Jetla**	**Mason**	**Radar**
Evaluators	**Wt.**	(Rows represent ranking for each criterion)			
Technical (Sam)	34.5	33	22	20	25
Commercial (Raj)	15.2	26	20	26	28
Operations (Mary)	21.4	27	29	21	23
Safety (Carol)	28.9	28	17	25	30
Final Rank %		**29.21**	**21.75**	**22.57**	**26.47**

On this occasion we formed four groups of specialists, each representing a criterion and evaluating the bids for its specialty.

1. Group leaders assigned weights to the criteria, which represented the company philosopphy. This is a critical step and we used *XpertUS* to minimize subjectivity.

2. Each group then used *XpertUS* and ranked the bids (candidates), considering only its specialty criterion. Each row in Table A shows the decision made by each group.

3. Finally, we used a weighted average technique to obtain the final ranking of candidates.

If you do not have access to *XpertUS*, use your best judgment or the matrix method.

NOTE: 1. Sum of all weights must add up to 100.
2. Each evaluator should distribute 100 points among the candidates.
3. E.g.: Simco: 33 x 34.5 + 26 x 15.2 + 27 x 21.4 + 28 x 28.9 = 2921; = 29.21%

B. Decision-Consolidation

I will discuss this technique using a hypothetical beauty contest. For convenience, let us specify four male judges: *Tom, Joe, Harry,* and *David.* Finally we have the four candidates: *Mary, Sarah, Monica,* and *Sylvia.* Information is available for each candidate, for each criterion.

Examples of this type of decision-making would be board meetings, an Olympic figure skating event, recruiting, etc. Each judge would submit his/her independent ranking of candidates, considering all criteria, using *XpertUS* or another technique. Thus we need to consolidate their decisions. We refer to this process as *decision-consolidation.*

The actual consolidated rankings can be obtained using one of two techniques:

B-1: The *Total-Point* Technique

This is similar to the technique discussed above in *criteria-consolidation,* except that we are consolidating the rankings of the evaluators.

Method B-1: Decision-Consolidation – Total-Point			
Contestants > >	**Mary**	**Sarah**	**Monica**	**Sylvia**
Judges	(Values represent ranking by each judge)			
Tom	17	19	39	25
Joe	25	28	27	20
Harry	17	29	26	28
David	19	33	32	16
	78.00	109.00	124.00	89.00
Final Ranking %	**19.50**	**27.25**	**31.00**	**22.25**

NOTE: 1. Each evaluator distributes 100 points among all the candidates;
2. Add points assigned to each candidate (e.g. Mary =78);
3. Add total points achieved by all candidates (78+109+124+89 = 400);
4. Consolidated points for each is the percentage of the total.
   (e.g. Mary = 100 x 78/400 = 19.50%)

B-2: The *Rank-Frequency* Technique

The base data is obtained from the *total-point* technique.

Here we are not concerned with the points gained by each candidate; we are concerned with the *rank* achieved by each candidate.

If there were four candidates, the first-ranked would get four points, while the last-ranked would get one point. If there were six candidates, the first-ranked would get six points, etc.

Now we add the points to determine the final ranking.

Method B-2: Decision Consolidation – Rank-Frequency				
Contestants > >	**Mary**	**Sarah**	**Monica**	**Sylvia**
Judges	(Each value represents the rank of each contestant)			
Tom	1	2	4	3
Joe	2	4	3	1
Harry	1	4	2	3
David	2	4	3	1
	6.00	14.00	12.00	8.00
Final Ranking %	**15.00**	**35.00**	**30.00**	**20.00**

NOTE: 1. Add total points achieved by all candidates (6+14+12+8 = 40);
2. Consolidated points for each is the percentage of the total.
(e.g. Mary = 100 x 6 /40 = 15.00%)

Note that in this example, the two techniques give different rankings, although this would not always be the case.

—◆—

The d*ecision-consolidation* technique is not suitable for evaluations of bids that have specialized criteria. Consider the *pump station* example where teams were assembled with specialists from technical, operational, safety, and financial areas. The *decision-consolidation* method requires people from the *financial* group to pass a value judgment on *technical* issues, and people from *safety* to render an opinion on *operational* issues. This is counter-productive to the evaluation.

Peer-evaluation Techniques

Examples of the need for "peer evaluation" would be in distributing bonuses, selecting a leader, etc., where individuals of a team decide to evaluate themselves. Within *XpertUS* this is referred to as "Peer Evaluation."

For example, if a research team were required to distribute the annual bonus among the team, the process would be:

1. The team would agree on a set of criteria.
2. Each member of the team would evaluate the team, including himself/herself, using *XpertUS*. They *must* all use the same criteria.
3. Now the team leader would use the "peer-evaluation" module of *XpertUS* to determine the distribution.

NOTE: Before starting the candidate evaluation, the team may use the "criteria-consolidation" technique to assign criteria weights.

Fourteen

Collaborative Negotiations

"Every battle is won before it is fought."

— Sun Tzu

Anything we would ever want or need is owned or controlled by someone else. Therefore, to get anything on our terms, we have to negotiate. Even when buying a fixed-price item, we negotiate time, terms, delivery, volume, warranty, add-ons, or any of the countless other things that are involved in a sale.

Negotiating is all about making decisions. This chapter deals with the Structure, Characteristics and Tactics that form the basis for negotiating.

A. Structure

Any negotiation should be structured around the following three stages:

1. Anchoring—establishing wants and needs (positions and interests)
2. Gathering information
3. Reaching a compromise, based on *perceived* values

1. Anchoring—Establishing wants and needs

Do not get into a negotiation where the *interests* of the two parties are not the same. There is not much point in a fisherman trying to negotiate with the fish; they have different interests. The fish wants to stay alive, while the fisherman wants to make a meal of it. So start by identifying needs and wants, and be prepared to listen, even if it is painful to hear what is being said.

In a negotiation, the two parties can have the same *interests*, and yet have *positions* that are 180° apart. Both terrorists and governments want justice, but each takes a different path to achieve this. The primary objective of any negotiation is to move away from the *positions* toward the *interests*. Remember, you can have anything you want, if you ensure that the other side gets what they want. However, it is an error to assume that the other side wants the same things you want.

In 1979, the Egyptians and Israelis sat across the negotiating table— the issue was the Sinai Peninsula. The Sinai had been a disputed region for centuries before Egypt gained sovereignty over it. Then Israel captured it during the 1967 war. Now Egypt wanted it back. Israel, on the other hand, realized that giving up the Sinai desert would pose an unacceptable threat to their security. It seemed a hopeless deadlock. They had apparently incompatible positions.

Yet, when the negotiators looked deeper they recognized that the interests of both parties revolved around *peace, security and sovereignty*. So they finally arrived at a settlement acceptable to both parties. Israel would hand over the Sinai to the Egyptians, and the Egyptian flag would fly over the entire region. However, it would be demilitarized.

Arguing over *positions* is futile; however, discussing *positions* is highly productive. It provides an anchor.

2. Gathering information
The purpose of gathering information is to formulate one's own strategy, and also to be able to predict the opponent's likely response.

Henry Kissinger reiterated Sun Tzu's words in a different form: "Before we enter a negotiation, we should know exactly what our opponent's strategy is."

For example, let us say you decide to buy a used car, advertised for $30,000. You make a low-ball offer of $22,000, conscious that you might get an angry response. But to your surprise, the other side accepts. What is your likely reaction? You would immediately think:

1. I could have done better!
2. There must be something wrong with this vehicle!

This shows that responses are predictable. If you are a good negotiator, and have adequate preparation, you should be able to predict responses from the other side.

3. Reaching a compromise, based on *perceived* values.

3.1 PERCEIVED VALUE
A friend recently asked me how much our house was worth. It appeared to be a simple question. He thought I was being evasive when I offered the following explanation.

I.   There is an *emotional* value. I would not move unless someone offered me a ridiculously high price. It is our ancestral home and has a sentimental value; besides, I like it.

II. The *market* value is what someone would pay if I put it up for sale without any rush to sell it.

III. There is a *recovery* value determined by my cost, relocation expense, etc., if I have to sell but do not wish to lose on the deal.

IV. It has a *fire-sale* value if I have to move in a hurry.

V.   The *appraised* value, used by the mortgage company.

VI. There is the *taxable* value, the amount at which the house is appraised by the local authorities for taxation purposes.

VII. Finally there is the *replacement* value, which is set by insurance companies.

My friend needed to be more specific. When you are negotiating, you must decide what something is worth to *you* — establish the value!

True, perception is not reality. However, it is our perceptions that drive our decisions.

3.2 OBJECTIVES AND CONSEQUENCES

The two most common reasons why so many people lose out at negotiations are:

1. They lose sight of the objective. The objective must remain the primary focus.
2. They are not cognizant of the consequences of a disagreement.

In the Gulf Air example (P-68), had the company negotiated astutely, they would have recognized Dubai's potential and could have eliminated a future competitor while incorporating their rival's savvy. Instead they were driven to mediocrity. Similarly, had Encyclopedia Britannica (EB) been responsive to Microsoft's offer of a joint venture, EB would not have had to face a formidable adversary (P-69). In both of the above examples, the companies should have been cognizant of the potential consequences of rejecting the offers. Compare these with the strategies used by the airbrush manufacturer (P-84).

3.3 WHO SHOULD NEGOTIATE?

When I was on an assignment in Abu Dhabi, we needed to replace a compressor. But we wanted to get some concessions from the vendor. Hassan, the compressor engineer, produced a very detailed paper on the problems and on what we should try to get. The director of engineering asked Hassan to negotiate with the vendor. It was a complete fiasco. We left nearly $200,000 on the table. Hassan lost sight of the objective because he was focused on showing off his knowledge.

This irritated the vendor, who consequently did not concede anything.

In the corporate world, there are two common misconceptions:

1. The person who knows the most about the subject should do the negotiating.

2. The supervisor is better at negotiating than a subordinate.

Yes, by all means have the experts gather the finer points of the subject; but the actual negotiating should be assigned to a trained person. When you negotiate, facts and figures are only a small part of the game plan. Perceptions, human emotions, values, and ego play a much bigger role. Remember Colin Powell's comment about experts: "Experts often possess more data than judgment"!

Always conduct your business in accordance with established business norms. In addition to complying with the law, your conduct must also meet high ethical standards.

3.4 FLEXIBILITY

The negotiating process entails the *substance* and the *relationships*. The latter will be dictated by *aggressive* (*hard*) or *collaborative* (*soft*) styles. If you were negotiating with your employer or your neighbor, it would be prudent to resort to a *soft* style.

When negotiating, you are going to have to concede on some issues so as to get agreement on others which are critical to your position. You need to know how to manage these. Do not be inflexible or you are bound to come away without an agreement.

Since negotiating is all about *feelings*, start asking for a lot, and then grant many concessions. It is important to let the opponent feel he/she has done well in the negotiations. Remember, their expectations at the beginning of the negotiations may have changed by the end; but they must feel that this was a good replacement for their original requirement. Furthermore, if they feel you behaved in a reasonable manner, they will have less of a problem giving in.

Never reduce the negotiation to one issue. If you do, there has to be a winner and a loser. At the end of any negotiation, all parties want to walk away feeling that they came out winning, or at least that this was a win-win outcome. Therefore, you must start with the willingness to let the other side *feel* that they achieved most, if not all, of what they wanted.

Always pretend that you are a reluctant buyer/seller. Always be prepared to walk away. Don't go into a negotiation saying, "I am going to get this contract somehow!"

Sometimes it makes sense to leave some issues open. In the Gulf War (1990-91), the Iraqis were defeated, but there was never a formal surrender. The U.S. agreed to end the war; they were never insistent on getting a piece of paper indicating a formal surrender. The objective was to liberate Kuwait, and that objective had been achieved.

At other times, it even makes sense to concede on principles. In the case of Robert Hanssen (the spy/traitor), the FBI agreed (negotiated) not to seek the death penalty, in exchange for full disclosure of all his activities.

In Appendix 5, I present an interesting case study.

B. Characteristics

The critical characteristics of any negotiation are:

1. Power
Power to influence or intimidate the other party is extremely valuable in a negotiation. Power comes in four distinct forms:

  A. *Power of Expertise.* People will respect and trust those with expertise or information.

B. *Power of Principle:* People will follow a person who has consistent values, even if they might be opposed to some of these values.

C. *Power of Position:* Power bestowed by a title or position, with the power to reward or punish. Negotiate in your own territory. This gives you a perceived power.

D. *Power of Stardom:* Sports stars and movie stars have a fanatical following.

Negotiate from a position of strength. There is nothing wrong with subtle intimidation. Although it may not sound noble to admit it, we capitalize on our strength at every opportunity. Even the White House is known to have resorted to this type of tactic. When President George Bush (Sr.) was planning to attack Iraq (1991), there was much backdoor diplomacy. He warned Saddam Hussein that if Iraq opted for germ warfare, the U.S. would use the nuclear option. It worked.

2. Personality Styles

"Like-minded" people agree on most things. The flip side to this is that people with different personalities would find it difficult to agree. Identify your opponent's personality as soon as possible. An astute negotiator realizes that to reach a compromise he/she has to adjust to the opponent's personality. We can categorize negotiators as belonging to one of four different personalities:

A. *Agreeable:* This person does his/her very best to ensure that everyone is happy. Rather than win, they seek agreement and even accept losses.

B. *Pragmatic:* This is a bottom-line person. Driven by information and opinions. Quick to respond and decide. Conscious of the value of time. Believes in winning at any cost. Demands that the other guy loses.

C. *Extrovert:* Enjoys the excitement. Does not care about the details. Will buy with emotions and then justify with logic. Is assertive, and loves to take a position, and influence others toward that position. Loses sight of the objective.

D. *Analytical:* Very organized and orderly. Likes specifics. Can never have too much information. Is a sequential thinker.

3. Body language

Wherever possible, negotiate face-to-face; body movements provide important clues. Note that only changes in movement are significant. However, these evolve over time, and also depend on the culture.

It is important to sign off on an agreement with a handshake. Arabs first shake hands, have a meal, and then start the negotiations. Westerners negotiate first, then shake hands, and finally, sit down for a meal.

C. Tactics

The tactics used in a negotiation will determine the outcome of the negotiation.

In Appendix 6, I provide a comprehensive set of guidelines and tactics to help improve negotiating skills.

THE "PI" RULE: Separate the *people* from the *issues*, and the *positions* from the *interests*. A *collaborative* negotiator separates the people from the issues, and encourages the other side to do the same.

Negotiators are people! Deal with the people issues first. Often perception is the difference. Most people will defend their religious beliefs most fervently, and even justify them. Yet, if they were born to another religion, they would probably defend that religion just as fervently.

Part Two

The 7-Step Guide To Bulletproof Your Decisions

The 7-Step Guide

The Seven Steps to Effective Decision-Making

1. Study the problem and clearly define your objective.

2. Identify all relevant criteria and define the prerequisites (limiting prerequisites).

3. Extract obligatory criteria.

4. Creatively identify all available candidates (options) that meet all prerequisites.

5. Gather information on candidates—pros and cons, pertaining to the criteria, and also add any new criteria.

6. Assign weights to the obligatory criteria.

7. Rank candidates.

N ow that you understand the basics of decision-making and know how to use *XpertUS*, you are ready to apply the seven steps to making a good decision, whatever your problem.

Let us consider each of the steps.

1. STUDY THE PROBLEM AND DEFINE YOUR OBJECTIVE

Very often, one is likely to think that one has a good idea of the problem. Maybe; but to understand the problem is not necessarily to understand the objective. When trying to solve a problem, one needs to have an unambiguous objective. Try to review the problem. Here are some fundamental questions that one should ask (see box—p. 152). Clarity of objective deals with framing the problem.

It is difficult to generate a list of criteria if the objective is vague. A good example of vagueness prevails in the gas industry, where the term *capacity* has many different definitions. There is design

151

capacity, certified capacity, firm capacity, operational capacity, seasonal capacity, etc., each with a very specific meaning. Thus, it is not enough for management to say that we need to increase *capacity*. The objective has to be more specific. How can you increase something if you don't know what is expected of you? It is imperative that we be clear about our primary objective.

> ## Defining the Objective — Basic Questions
> • What is the problem?
> • Is this a problem?
> • Why is a solution required?
> • Who is affected?
> • When did it first manifest itself?
> • How does it manifest itself?
> • What triggers this problem?
> • What are the consequences?
> • Under what conditions does this occur?
> • Is this a transient or recurring problem?
> • Are there obvious causes?
> • Is a solution likely to be cost effective?

- Ask the typical politician about his/her objective on a congressional vote—on subsidized housing, for example—and he/she would tell you a story; but his/her primary objective would be to ensure that he/she gets elected.

- When President George W. Bush imposed tariffs on steel imports, was the primary objective an issue of *national concern* or was it *political expediency?*

- If a drop in sales revenue is negatively impacting bottom-line profits, don't rush to push for increase in sales. A brainstorming session produced these options: *Reduce development costs; Reduce production costs; Improve customer service; Improve warranties; New technologies; Increase capacity; New advertising & marketing; New distribution techniques; Expand into new markets; Acquire a competitor; Lobby for new regulations; Add new products; Add new services; Sales incentives; Modify the product; New pricing, etc.*

- If you define your problem as "how to increase the energy supply by the year 2010", you will overlook the problem of "how to decrease the consumption of energy".

- If you define a problem as "where to build a school" you will limit your options, for an effective solution. If defined as "where to find more classroom space", the question would generate creative solutions such as *converting a warehouse to a classroom* or *using a bingo hall for daytime classes.*

- When President Ronald Reagan was elected, the U.S. foreign policy was based on *fighting communism.* However, once Reagan took office, he redefined this policy to *spreading democracy.* There was a marked difference—under *fighting communism,* the U.S. was supporting and financing dictators and propping up brutal regimes, in exchange for cooperation in the battle against communism.

- Strategists at Burger King (B-K) noticed the move to a healthy lifestyle: increase in sales of vitamins, whole-food stores, and the growth in the fitness industry. Accordingly, B-K developed a "flame-broiled" chicken burger, and spent millions of dollars to launch it, thinking that society was becoming more health-conscious. Alas, it was a dismal failure! Why? Strategists at B-K started with a wrong premise—they assumed that the customer would go to a fast-food outlet for a healthy meal. This led to the erroneous objective of "adding a healthy meal to the menu". Surveys have shown the only reason people go to a fast-food restaurant is for a "fast, cheap, palatable" product to satisfy their hunger. B-K started with a bad assumption!

And it was not only B-K who got it wrong! There were others who rode this wagon—going the wrong way!
- ✓ McDonald's abandoned the "McLean" burger.
- ✓ Pizza Hut shelved the "low-fat" pizza.
- ✓ Kentucky Fried Chicken tried the "skinless" variety, and dropped it fast.

- The Army did a great job training their infantrymen to have superb "marksmanship" skills. Yet, surveys revealed that only 25% of infantrymen actually fired at the enemy! Subsequently a new objective was established, i.e., to provide "killing" skills. Six months later, the Army revealed that 100% of the infantrymen had fired at the enemy.

OBJECTIVE

Many businesses do not understand their real objective.

- A retail cosmetic store is not in the business of selling cosmetics. Its primary objective is to "give hope". When a lady walks into a cosmetics store, she is hoping not so much to buy cosmetics, as to look good.

- For most politicians, the primary objective is to get (re)elected. Serving the electorate is a tactical move.

- An auto repair shop is in the business of providing "assurance"; fixing cars is a tactical activity.

- A stockbroker is in the business of gathering and retaining assets. "Performance" is a tactical activity.

Remember Honda (p. 92)? They have never deviated from their strategic objective of building engines.

When considering purchasing your products, what do your customers want? Before you rush to say "price," remember that, while there are many "free" credit cards, American Express has 25 million credit card customers in the US alone. And AMEX is not cheap!

2. IDENTIFY ALL RELEVANT CRITERIA THAT WILL IMPACT YOUR PROBLEM AND DEFINE PREREQUISITES

I discussed criteria at length in Chapter 9. Look at the criteria and define any prerequisites. Remember, prerequisites apply to candidate selection and not to criteria selection—they are pre-qualifying factors. It is important to recognize that you will never come up with all the criteria on the first go. Earlier (p. 107), I discussed *prerequisites* and noted that they evolve from two separate sources.

Always try to state your criteria in positive terms. This will lead to less confusion and better judgment. Also try to be specific. *Room temperature* does not tell you what temperature is desirable.

Since you would reject any candidate that does not meet the pre-requisites, it is imperative that you pay close attention to the assumptions governing prerequisites, as you might exclude a perfectly suitable candidate.

3. Extract Obligatory Criteria

If you do not have access to *XpertUS*, then you need to do the best you can with *common sense and experience*. Sadly, you will not do a good job, not because you are incompetent, but simply because of inherent human subjectivity and limitations. Wherever possible I recommend you use *XpertUS* to select the *obligatory* (evaluation) criteria. Unless you are an experienced decision-maker, I recommend that you do not include candidates at this time.

4. Creatively Identify All Available Candidates (options or solutions)

As I stressed earlier, do not jump to conclusions and think, *"My options are obvious."* Many experts who claim to have the answers have been proven wrong.

Remember the commissioner (1844) and the director (1899) of the Patent Office, who recommended that the Patent Office be closed down, because everything that could be invented had been invented and there was no longer any real need for such an office?

Don't forget to use the *aim-preset* technique to find all available candidates. Your final solution is only as good as your best candidate.

5. GATHER INFORMATION PERTAINING TO YOUR CANDIDATES

Start by looking at each of the candidates and list the pros and cons as they apply to each criterion. Set up a judgment table as shown. Be descriptive in your entries.

Judgment Table			
Candidates >>> Criteria	Cand-1	Cand-2	Cand-3
Crit-1			
Crit-2			
Crit-3			
Crit-4			

Pay particular attention to the quality of the information. Too often people make wild guesses, which become "fact" as they move from person to person.

When you start identifying the pros and cons, you have to gather information. It is imperative that you question the information being provided to you (see box, P-157).

Often, during the information-gathering stage, you will identify new criteria that need to be considered. These must be added to your original criteria list.

Beware of experts who claim that it cannot be done. I cited many examples of experts who made mistakes. I repeat my rule on experts:

When a recognized expert says that something is possible, he is almost always right; but when he states that something is impossible, he is likely to be wrong.

I caution you not to cut corners, especially if a bad decision is likely to have serious consequences. Always build a table for the candidates and write down the pros and cons. It does not take long and will be of enormous help to you.

6. ASSIGN WEIGHTS TO THE OBLIGATORY CRITERIA

This step is vital for successful decision-making. *XpertUS* is ideally suited for this operation.

Questions to ask during information gathering

- Is the source of the information legal, moral, and ethical?
- Are the measurements credible?
- Is the source/person reliable?
- Does the provider have a conflict of interest?
- Perishability—will the information be valid for the period under consideration?
- Is the problem serious enough to request further verification of information?
- Is the information relevant to the objective under consideration?
- Beware of eyewitness accounts or "I heard this from a reliable source." Seek definitive proof wherever possible. When did a jury accept an eyewitness account over a laboratory report?

If you do not have access to *XpertUS*, you will have to use your judgment or one of the less effective methods.

Note that criteria weights should represent the decision-maker's (or the company's) philosophy or value system.

7. RANK CANDIDATES

Wherever possible, use the *XpertUS* technique.

Caution! You might not be happy when you see the final ranking. Sometimes it is not what you expected.

157

A friend of mine was dating three girls at the same time and had a problem deciding which one he should select for his wife. I ran this through *XpertUS* and when the rankings were presented to him, he was unhappy. Why?

Though he used criteria applicable to a future wife, he was still visualizing the dating relationship and its associated pleasures. It has often been said that the girl you like to date would not necessarily make the ideal wife.

Sensitivity Analysis

When conducting an evaluation, watch for a condition I refer to as a *top-skewed* scenario. Consider a beauty contest where you assigned thirty percent to *facial beauty*. It turns out that all the girls are very beautiful and there is not much that separates them. We call this a *top-skewed* scenario. Thus, we remove *facial beauty* from the evaluation. In Chapter 11, I explained how to handle a problem of this type.

You may think that decision-making is a lot of work, but you need to consider the cost of a bad decision. Barry Smart (a human resources specialist) indicated that hiring an employee who makes $100K and losing him/her after a year amounts to a real loss of about $300K. Now you must decide if it is worth a little time and effort to get it right.

Even if you think you are very good at making decisions, would there not be some value in checking out an important decision using *XpertUS*? Would it not give an additional degree of confidence?

Part Three

Applications & Case Studies

Introduction

Decision-making embraces every facet of our lives. It does not matter whether you are in education, healthcare, transportation, energy, telecommunication, finance, marketing, pharmaceuticals or geopolitics, you will make crucial decisions.

Here are some of the applications where *XpertUS* can be applied with tremendous benefits:

- Selecting a consultant; contractor; vacation spot;
- Real Estate—buying a house or relocating;
- Insurance—deciding on a provider and on how much insurance to purchase;
- Timing an activity—getting married; starting a family;
- Marketing a product—deciding on an advertising medium;
- Human Resources—hiring, downsizing, performance evaluation, exit interviews;
- Site Selection—International Olympic Commission;
- Beauty contests and modeling agencies;
- Allocating funds—budgeting; charity giving;
- Coaching—selecting a team or recruiting a player;
- Elections—identifying the best candidate for office;
- Forming a team or selecting a project leader;
- Rating agencies;

- Bid evaluations and purchasing;
- Security services—deciding on appropriate solutions;
- Scheduling priorities—putting first things first;
- Newspaper editors—deciding which articles should be published;
- Managing customers—sales-force monitoring;
- Marital problems—identifying root causes;
- Training in the art of decision-making.

Some of the more popular applications are discussed in detail with a list of applicable criteria. These criteria were developed in association with specialists in each of the fields. In some cases, actual case studies are presented, while in others I provide guidelines and typical criteria.

One

Purchasing — Bid Evaluation

Even if procurement is your specialty, you need to learn about decision-making, since procurement involves decision-making. The methodology I present will help you reach an optimum decision.

Bids or tenders are issued when buying or selling goods or services. When you sell a product, in general it is the end of a transaction, without any further commitments. In such cases, there is no need for a lengthy evaluation. Cases where there are issues such as form of payment, delivery, warrantees, or liabilities, merit a more detailed evaluation, as discussed herein.

This section deals primarily with what happens when you acquire goods or services. This critical decision-making process has two fundamental requirements: o*bjectivity* and *transparency*. These were discussed in Chapter 1. Indeed, even if the selection process is subject to strict monitoring, proving this to the public and to monitoring authorities is a daunting task.

In evaluating bids, the most important steps are:
- Identifying the relevant criteria
- Assigning meaningful weights

To do this effectively, one needs a technique that is reliable and consistent.

Most companies start by hiring a consultant or an expert (maybe in-house) to develop a *scope of work*. The consultant will then identify the criteria for the evaluation and recommend a list of bidders (candidates). Even though the consultant is *not* an expert in bid evaluation, almost always the client hands over the entire process to this person. This is a big mistake, since bid evaluation requires a thorough understanding of the process and governing factors.

The *persuasive leader*: How often have you seen the coordinator do all the work? He/she might have assigned criteria weights *a priori*. Soon the rest of the team begins to notice he/she is setting the tone to sway the decision to suit his/her preference, yet they stay silent and non-committal; it takes a lot of effort to coordinate an evaluation process. In nearly thirty bid evaluations that I have participated in, I have seen this pattern in every case without a single exception. Most participants have no *ownership* in the final outcome; they are just waiting to complete the process and return to their routine work.

Unfortunately, we have been held hostage by the *matrix* method, which has been the only option available to decision-makers for evaluating bids. This is woefully inadequate. In Chapter 10, I discussed the frailty of the matrix method.

Often a team performs a bid-evaluation. The team consists of a representative (specialist) for each of the evaluation criteria. Where necessary, each specialist member of the team forms his/her own small group; the groups now represent areas of specialized know-how. Thus, in addition to the seven steps, bid-evaluation requires subsequent consolidation. Different consolidation techniques add further confusion.

How you *consolidate* an evaluation to arrive at a final ranking depends on the manner in which the evaluation is conducted. In chapter 13, I discussed the two basic methods of consolidation.

Other Considerations

Many organizations have their own procedures for tenders. It is not my intention to lay down a detailed procedure, but to draw your attention to important issues.

THE TWO-PART BID SYSTEM

Some public organizations require bids be submitted in two separate sealed envelopes, namely, *technical* and *commercial* bids. The *technical* bid is evaluated with no consideration of commercial terms. The organization is also required to develop an in-house cost estimate of the project. First, bidders are ranked on the technical evaluation. Then, the *commercial* bid of the top-ranked bidder is opened and compared to the in-house estimate. If discussions do not produce an agreement, negotiations are initiated with the second-ranked bidder.

THE HI-LO REJECTION TECHNIQUE

Some companies invite a minimum of seven bidders and then reject the most expensive and the least expensive. This is usually done when the company has no idea of what the project should cost.

INVITING BIDDERS

If the objective is not defined clearly, it is easy to invite bidders with totally different skill sets. Always ensure that the candidates pass the *prerequisites* test. If you are looking to purchase a family car, do not include a two-door sports coupe in your comparison.

Sometimes, certain coordinators invite *fillers* (i.e., bidders who are highly inferior or those known to be prohibitively expensive) to ensure their preferred candidate wins. The evaluation process is then simply a smoke screen.

CLARIFICATIONS, REFERENCES, AND SITE VISITS

At the very outset of a tender, there is at least one bid clarification meeting where the bidders get an opportunity to ask questions. This information is transmitted to all bidders. It is imperative that the coordinator handles all such clarifications. The same single source responsibility applies with respect to references and site visits.

If you screen the bidders and invite bidders of the same quality, your evaluation should demonstrate congruency among the bidders. A good evaluation technique should provide decisions that are objective, accurate, transparent, and consistent over time.

STEP 1 — PREPARING & ISSUING BIDS

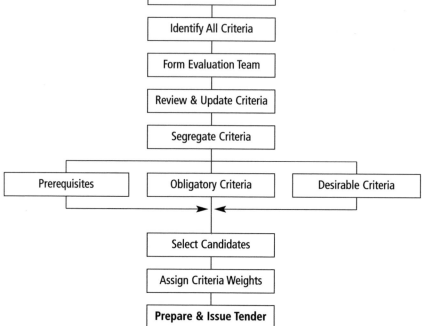

STEP 2 — EVALUATING BIDS

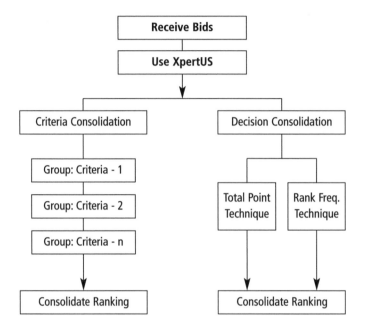

Two

Human Resources

*"63% of all hiring decisions are made during
the first 4.3 minutes of an interview."*
— Society of Human Resources Managers

The Human Resources Department (HR) plays a vital role in every company. In addition to the traditional HR functions, management is increasingly turning to HR for maintaining records, providing services and facilities, and ensuring compliance. HR is involved in a multitude of decision-making activities (see box). In most instances, some manager or group of managers makes these decisions *as they see fit.* This inevitably adds a high degree of *subjectivity.* Recent publications have highlighted glaring failures in the HR industry and have pointed out the need to make better decisions. Many companies have a high turnover of personnel—often employees leaving due to disenchantment. Companies have invested a considerable amount of money in some of these people.

The HR Department

- Hiring (Resumes & Interviews)
- Resource Allocation, Selecting Teams and Managers
- Downsizing, Layoffs and Turnover Analyses
- Determining Career Development and Training Needs
- Performance Evaluation & Bonus Payments
- Exit Interviews

XpertUS provides a method by which HR can manage and defend decisions. *Transparency* and *Objectivity* are indelible hallmarks of *XpertUS*. While the decision-making process is basically the same in all HR applications, the focus and the emphasis change, depending on the objective. Below are discussions of the various applications.

I expect most HR personnel to reject *XpertUS* at first. This is natural. It will appear to be a lot of work for a small benefit. However, *hiring the wrong person* or the loss of a *disenchanted employee* is not a trivial matter. If the HR function is viewed as important, then it only makes sense to use *XpertUS* to make optimum decisions.

Barry Smart, an HR consultant and a psychologist, stated that hiring and then losing a professional making $100K a year actually would cost a company about $300K, when you factor in relocation, training, loss of competitive edge, etc. By any measure, this is significant.

— THE HIRING PROCESS

1. THE RESUME

The first step in the hiring process is a review of the resume. Is it consistent with the job description? Invariably, many applicants—possibly too many to interview—will meet the basic requirements, and it is not uncommon for HR to eliminate candidates simply because there are too many. I suggest that you follow the seven steps. It is perfectly safe to develop a shortlist based on the results of *XpertUS*.

I have provided an extensive list of generic criteria; the user should add his/her own specific criteria as applicable.

2. THE INTERVIEW

We all agree that there is no substitute for an interview. But what is the true purpose of the interview?

Whether we would admit it or not, during the interview process we try to determine if the prospect shares our values. Additionally, we try to find out if this person is who he/she claims to be, has the knowledge and the experience reflected in the resume, etc. If we are really desperate, we are likely to be less demanding. If we pay less than the prevalent market rate, we are likely to be more accommodating. These are highly subjective decisions.

XpertUS is perfect for this type of decision-making because it helps you to minimize the subjective influence. In fact, an *XpertUS* analysis could protect HR from a potential discrimination lawsuit. If a candidate who fails to get a job claims he/she had been rejected unfairly, *XpertUS* is adequate proof of the use of a structured and disciplined selection methodology.

Criteria used in the *interview* process are different from the ones used in the *resume* evaluation.

HR: Hiring

- Qualifications
- Age
- Sex
- Citizenship
- Languages
- Salary expectation
- Total years of work
- Present employment
- Direct work experience
- Related work experience
- Family status
- Foreign exposure
- Willingness to travel
- Communication skills
- Temperament
- Self-motivation
- Presentation skills
- Availability
- Aspirations/Ambition
- Management potential
- Personality
- Team player
- Physical impediments
- Political affiliations
- Religious affiliations
- Writing skills
- Other relevant skills

We tested this technique on several occasions and found it to be extremely reliable. Recently a chip-manufacturing company used *XpertUS* in their Fresh-Graduate hiring program.

171

— Resource Allocation, Selecting Team Leaders and Managers

Often companies assemble a team to undertake important tasks on a tight schedule. Typically, such a team is formed by a senior executive, who rarely pays attention to the current commitments of the people under consideration; he/she tends to use dictatorial powers.

HR: Selecting a Leader

- Unwavering courage
- Controlled temperament
- Sense of justice
- Creative
- Persistent
- Affirmative
- Good listener
- Organizational skills
- Decisiveness
- Willing to do more
- Pleasing personality
- Sympathetic/Understanding
- Detailed knowledge of task
- Willing to assume responsibility
- Inspires others
- Carries out instructions
- Free of other commitments
- Health
- Age
- Physical impediments
- Personal habits
- Other qualities

Having formed the team or task force, it is often necessary to appoint a leader. What is important to note is that the criteria that govern the selection of a leader or a manager are not the same as those which apply to the team selection process (see box).

Certain situations require staff reassignment. HR faces a difficult situation when creating a new department using persons within the organization. Here, the benefit to the new department must be weighed against the loss to the host department. These are very delicate situations to which management must pay serious attention. Almost always, *whom you know* determines the final outcome. *XpertUS* is ideal for this type of problem.

Similarly, fresh graduates are rotated within an organization to give them an opportunity to get to know the company. Then there comes a time when they need to be assigned to a department and possibly define their career within the organization. All too often, managers take this too lightly. They think, *"Well, if he doesn't fit in, we can move him elsewhere."* This is a waste of time and talent. With *XpertUS* it is possible to work with the individual to identify the best fit. HR should require that these young persons use *XpertUS* to rank their preferences. Then HR can assign them based on availability of space.

— PERFORMANCE EVALUATION and BONUS PAYMENTS

Everyone thinks, *I am as good as the next person;* yet, companies have to evaluate employee performance. This is a manager's nightmare. If not handled properly, it can lead to disenchantment and the possible loss of employees. The same arguments hold true when it comes to bonus payments. If you have any doubt, ask a manager how difficult the process is. *XpertUS* Peer Evaluation can be used to demonstrate to the employees that this process was carried out objectively. The risk of errors and disenchantment is greatly minimized.

HR: Performance Evaluation

• Teamwork
• Problem Solving
• Accountability
• Motivation
• Job Knowledge
• Planning & Organization
• Communication
• Work Quality
• Adaptability
• Attendance/Punctuality
• Discipline
• Added Value (Revenue)
• Work Output
• Responsiveness

Even if your company operates with *teams,* you can use *XpertUS* to rank the *teams.* Typically, members of a team are reluctant to criticize another member of the team. *XpertUS* filters out these weaknesses without creating conflicts.

— Promotion to a Supervisory Position

The evaluation for promotions is very similar in principle to a performance evaluation. However, there are other considerations: Will he/she be happy with the promotion? Is the person available? Would the new position be beyond the person's capacity? Recall *The Peter Principle*—it is easy to promote someone to a level higher than his/her true aptitude, where he/she fails to perform as expected.

General George Patton is one of America's most decorated war heroes. When he was recommended for an independent command, General George Marshall, Chief of Staff, said, "Patton is the best subordinate that the American Army has ever produced, but he would be the worst commander."

— Downsizing and Turnover Analyses

Downsizing is dictated by bottom-line profit motives. Many reputable organizations offer very tempting severance packages to encourage employees to accept voluntary severance. If this is offered across the board, invariably the best employees will take the offer, simply because they can easily get a job with one of the competitors. To circumvent this, some companies reserve the right of refusal. This, however, can become a very delicate issue. The other option is to selectively terminate employees. This, too, brings new problems. The company may be exposed to lawsuits on the grounds of unfair treatment. An employee can claim, even frivolously, that he/she was discriminated against. The cost of defending against such a lawsuit could be very high. It is also possible that a good employee is inadvertently terminated. Using *XpertUS*, the organization can minimize a company's exposure on both counts.

However, since *XpertUS* is based on hierarchical ranking, run *XpertUS* as though you are trying to identify who should be kept rather than who should be terminated. Those with the lowest points are the ones to be considered for termination.

— Career Development and Training

Who decides career development? In a large company, there is a career development officer. However, more often than not, it is the already overloaded HR officer who has to work on career development as well.

Ask any HR officer about the importance of career development and you will hear a beautiful narration, but it is the last thing on his/her mind, because he/she has to attend to more pressing issues. Remember the *urgent* vs. the *important.* Career development seldom gravitates from the *important* to the *urgent* until the CEO asks why the average age of his employees is 50-plus, and suddenly it is a problem that needs *urgent* attention.

How do we go about career development? Usually companies give employees a list of available courses and the employee, either alone or with a supervisor, selects those that are most relevant. Furthermore, most companies are in the habit of pushing all new-hires through the same training program regardless of their personal traits and career objectives. This procedure is woefully inadequate.

HR: Training Priorities

- Verbal skills
- Writing skills
- Hands-on experience
- Specialized knowledge
- Team building skills
- Leadership potential
- Management training
- Presentation skills
- Language skills
- Strategic planning
- Personality building
- Problem-solving
- Visualization
- Computer skills
- Survival skills
- Persistence skills
- Psychiatric help
- Physical fitness
- Didactic training
- Stress management
- Creative thinking
- Sales techniques
- Listening skills
- Humility
- Aggression control

If the manager is allowed to dominate the process, there is inevitable subjectivity toward that manager's own specialty. If left to the employee, he/she will be utterly lost as to priorities.

Before starting the process, it is necessary to write a *career development objective* to help determine criteria. Also, a time-span must be identified. There is no point in taking a course that would help you ten years from now. Here is a career development objective for Joe White:

Joe White has been a data-entry clerk with the company for six months. He is attending the local community college to become a software developer. We would like Joe to become a Visual Basic Programmer within twelve months. He needs to work on his writing and listening skills. He also has to be trained in management skills, as he will have three data-entry assistants working for him. Furthermore, he does not know much about teamwork and he needs to learn about workplace ethics.

Now it is time to develop Joe's *Career Plan.* We recommend you use *XpertUS* to develop a proper plan for Joe. Let Joe participate in his career development. Let him and his supervisor run the program and discover what Joe's training priorities should be. In this instance it is not necessary to have any criteria, as long as the objective is clearly defined. You can operate purely on candidates (the courses). However, if there are multiple objectives, it is necessary to set up a criteria table.

Special consideration should be given to candidate hierarchy—one cannot take a course in advanced programming without first completing basic programming. The employee must meet the prerequisites of the particular training program.

— THE EXIT INTERVIEW

If you believe in the adage, o*ur employees are our greatest assets,* the departure of a valued employee is a serious loss. Companies invest much time and money training their employees; thus losing a key employee is of major concern. It is worse if he/she joins a rival company or sets up his/her own company. Many companies have exit interviews in an effort to understand why people leave. When dealing with exit interviews, many have an attitude that can be aptly described in Shakespeare's words, "... *is more honored in the breach than the observance.*"

What is the real purpose of an exit interview? At least, we pretend that such a thing benefits the company and the employee. The employee gets an opportunity to vent his/her frustrations, while the company gets a chance to file a piece of paper. Unless the employee specifically gives his/her reasons for departure, this

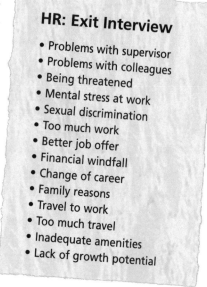

HR: Exit Interview
- Problems with supervisor
- Problems with colleagues
- Being threatened
- Mental stress at work
- Sexual discrimination
- Too much work
- Better job offer
- Financial windfall
- Change of career
- Family reasons
- Travel to work
- Too much travel
- Inadequate amenities
- Lack of growth potential

type of interview serves little purpose. The fact that most employees do not wish to *burn any bridges* limits what the company can learn from the exit interview.

Here is how you would conduct an exit interview, using *XpertUS*.

Let the employee run *XpertUS* and express his/her reasons for leaving. This will identify the reasons for the employee's departure from his/her standpoint, without any influence from the company. This is a very important step. Most employees are reluctant to criticize the company, but *XpertUS* will narrow down his/her reasons. Since *XpertUS* does not ask any questions directly, the employee will not be reticent about expressing his/her feelings.

Now the HR representative should have the formal interview—*a chat-session.* HR would present the probable top five reasons and try to get the departing employee to elaborate on these.

I recommend that companies offer a financial incentive to employees to encourage them to attend the exit interview.

XpertUS has resolved many arguments during decision-making. Managers realize they cannot simply think of the needs of their department, but must think also of the needs of the company. In addition, they must try to minimize subjectivity during the selection process. *XpertUS* can be a lifesaver to the human resources manager.

Remember what Peter Drucker said: "Chances are that 66% of your company's hiring decisions will prove to be mistakes within the first twelve months."

Three

Personal — Selecting a Partner/Spouse

In the late '80s, one out of every three marriages ended in a divorce. Today, one in every two marriages ends in a divorce. Ironically, nearly 80% of those who get divorced re-marry within three years.

Marriage is possibly the most important decision we make. We must therefore make the best possible decision.

There are many books on how to make your marriage work once you get married. However, it would make sense to pick the right partner in the first place. We have listed criteria that are important in selecting a partner. You may wish to add your own. I suggest you try to find out what is really important to you in a partner. Run *XpertUS* with your criteria. Thereafter, you can analyze the candidates.

In 1999, I was in Mexico City, and met with Ricardo and Jose, who were to develop some marketing material for *XpertUS*.

After several meetings, Jose jokingly asked me if I could help Ricardo decide on something personal. It turned out that Ricardo was dating three girls at the same time and having a hard time deciding on "Miss Right". This was an ideal use for the 7-step guide, and I agreed to help.

The 7-Step Guide

STEP 1: Study the problem, and clearly define your objective

We set the objective as *"selecting a spouse."*

STEP 2: Write down all the criteria, define the prerequisites, and set limiting values

Here the first step was to list criteria that pertained to a spouse, as opposed to a girlfriend. To my surprise he gave me thirty criteria (see box).

Since he had already selected the candidates, we removed the following from the criteria list: *Race/Heritage; Religion; Height compatibility; Weight; Age compatibility.*

STEP 3: Extract the *obligatory* criteria

We were now left with twenty-five criteria, still too many. So we ran *XpertUS* to segregate criteria. Being such a personal issue, Ricardo had a tough time admitting to certain preferences. Remember, our objective was to select the candidate who best reflected Ricardo's criteria, with due consideration to criteria weightings.

To our surprise, 87% of the weights were in twelve criteria. Hence, we settled on these obligatory criteria.

STEP 4: Select all available candidates (options) who meet all prerequisites

We already had the candidates.

STEP 5: Gather information on candidates; also any new criteria

Ricardo was able to provide this information quite easily.

STEP 6 : Assign weights to the *obligatory* criteria

We conducted this step along with step 7.

STEP 7: Rank candidates

Finally we conducted the ranking evaluation. The final ranking was as follows:

1. Maria Elena — 39.2%
2. Consuela — 38.5%
3. Monica — 22.3%.

Ricardo looked at me and said, *"Garbage; I like Monica most, and I know it."* This was what I was afraid of. After some discussion, it was apparent that Ricardo liked Monica's easygoing *sexy* style. She was always looking for a *good time.* I pointed out that these were not his criteria for a spouse. The ranking itself was too close to decide between Maria Elena and Consuela.

Note: Soon afterwards Ricardo stopped seeing Monica; the following year he married Maria Elena.

Four

Real Estate — Buying a Home

A home is possibly the most expensive purchase most of us will ever make. Yet, if you were to pause and think how you decided on your last home, you would agree that it was part analysis, but mostly emotional—just feeling good about the one you decided on. I am certain you would agree that we can, and should, do better.

STEP 1: Study the problem and clearly define your objective
First you sit with the realtor and discuss your objective. This is the *defining* phase.

STEP 2: Write down all the criteria and define the prerequisites and limiting values
Now identify your wants and needs regarding your dream house. These are *criteria*. You can specify as many criteria as you choose. At this time you must also identify the prerequisites and the limiting conditions.

STEP 3: Extract *obligatory* criteria
Run *XpertUS* to separate the criteria into two groups—*obligatory* criteria and *desirable* features. Of course, husbands and wives will argue forever on this issue. If they cannot agree, or if there are more than about fifteen criteria, run *XpertUS*, to identify the most relevant criteria.

Criteria for Buying a Home

- Size of house
- Total cost or cost per sq. ft.
- Cost of utilities
- Price of house + repairs
- Financing
- Taxes
- Resale potential
- Appreciation
- Proximity to buses
- Age of house
- Condition of house
- Size of yard
- Modern conveniences
- Pool
- Front appearance
- Number of rooms
- Floor-plan
- Proximity to work
- Quality of schools
- Proximity to schools
- Quality of neighborhood
- Size of garage
- Landscaping
- Type of neighbors
- Status of location
- Likelihood of floods
- City or county
- Quality of construction
- Quality of finish
- Availability (time)
- ... and other criteria

STEP 4: Select all available candidates (options) that meet all prerequisites

Submit the prerequisites to a database containing houses for sale (in the U.S. this would be a Multiple Listing Service) and select the houses that meet the prerequisites; these are the *candidates*.

STEP 5: Gather information on candidates; also any new criteria

Gather information pertaining to all the candidates. Build a table of pros and cons. Add any new criteria that may surface. Now tour the homes. Make notes for each of the criteria, but do not attempt to rank the candidates.

STEP 6: Assign weights to the *obligatory* criteria

Run *XpertUS* on the *obligatory* criteria and assign weights.

STEP 7: Rank candidates

Now you are ready to run *XpertUS* on the candidates.

XpertUS has resolved many arguments during decision-making, as it can help both the realtor and the buyer select the home that truly represents the buyer's desires and resources. Clients are convinced that they cannot have everything all the time—they have to give up somethings.

We tested this technique with eight clients and six of them made up their minds after the second tour. *XpertUS* is a bonanza for realtors! I urge you to try it out.

At a recent real estate training session, I asked Jane (a realtor) to imagine that she was purchasing a house. Note that Jane is married, has two kids (ages 8 and 6), and her husband works in the city as an engineer.

I asked her to tell me the five most important criteria in her search for a home for her family. Jane paused for a while and gave these criteria:
- Price
- Floor-plan
- Age of the house
- Distance to her husband's work place
- A location safe from flooding

Then I asked her if *safety* was of lower priority. She said, "Oh no, that is the most important thing." I said, "Yet you never even mentioned it!" She was somewhat embarrassed.

Then I asked her, "Would you like your kids to attend a school district that has a reputation for quality education?"

"Oh! Yes, I'd give up anything to give them a good education." Once again I looked at her with a puzzled grin, but I did not have to say it—she realized that she had not thought through her priorities. It was not that she had not thought about them. All of us try to conjure up a few criteria that come to mind, and stop there.

I have provided a host of criteria that some of the test subjects considered (see box). I invite you to select your criteria from this list and add any others.

Five

Buying an Automobile

The automobile is an integral part of the American lifestyle. Most of us have purchased at least one car. Many purchase a car every five to ten years.

Regardless of your emotions, why not test your decision using the 7-step technique?

STEP 1: Study the problem and clearly define your objective

Be very clear about the purpose for which you would use this vehicle: Main family vehicle; second vehicle; hauling large items; driving to the bus/train station; status symbol; vacation needs; etc.

Buying an Automobile

- Price
- Financing
- Fuel economy
- Engine power
- Maintenance cost/history
- Safety record
- Theft potential
- Cost of insurance
- Style/Appearance
- Basic features
- Cost of options
- Resale value
- Ease of driving
- Seating capacity
- Ease of parking
- Garage space needed
- 4-wheel drive
- Status symbol
- Reliability
- … and others

STEP 2: Write down all the criteria, define the prerequisites, and set limiting values

Use the list shown in the box and select criteria that reflect your needs. Do not forget to specify the prerequisites and also the limiting conditions.

STEP 3: Extract *obligatory* criteria

Since you are not likely to have more than about fifteen criteria, you may skip this step.

STEP 4: Select all available candidates (options) that meet all prerequisites

This is the most difficult step. Unless you are diligent, you are likely to include only candidates you are familiar with. I suggest you refer to some publications to get additional information.

STEP 5: Gather information on candidates; also any new criteria

Visit several car dealerships and search the Internet to gather as much information as possible. Do not forget to add any new criteria that you discover during your visits.

STEP 6: Assign weights to the *obligatory* criteria

Run *XpertUS* to assign criteria weights.

STEP 7: Rank candidates

Run *XpertUS* to rank criteria.

(Note: you can always do steps 6 and 7 simultaneously.)

Six

Career Guidance — Which Profession?

Surveys

1. We conducted an informal survey with the aid of a high school counselor and were surprised to note that only 32% of the graduating class had decided on a career or profession.

2. A survey by *Accounting Age* revealed that, out of six hundred accountants surveyed, 38% said they wish they had never gone into that profession.[13]

These two surveys tell us that there is an alarming level of uncertainty and disenchantment about career selection.

I have provided herein a set of criteria that applies to career choice. Additionally, I have provided a list of jobs as categorized by the U.S. Department of Labor (Appendix 7).

This is a good starting point for anyone. You can refine your search later. I recommend that you read other books on career guidance to further enhance your knowledge. However, *XpertUS* is still the best tool to help you make the final decision.

I present a case where a young Asian student wanted to decide on a career. He applied to two colleges and was accepted by

Criteria for Deciding on a Profession

- Natural aptitude
- Ability to learn a skill
- Adequate pre-qualifications
- Short-term income potential
- Long-term income potential
- Job security
- Job growth trends
- Location of job
- Language requirements
- Financial resources
- Serving the nation
- Excessive travel
- Work schedule/long hours
- Willing to be away from home
- Work from home
- Stress-free job
- Work under pressure
- Quick-response type work
- Frequent relocation
- Work in foreign countries
- Technical or scientific field
- Management aspirations
- Family needs
- Degree of specialization

both: UCLA Berkeley, for Physics, and Caltech, for Mathematics.

However, he had a strong desire to enter the priesthood, and had spent many nights agonizing over his future. Through a mutual friend, he was introduced to *XpertUS*. He used it three times, and on each occasion *XpertUS* ranked the priesthood as his future career. Today he is well on his way to serving God.

Seven

Career Guidance — Which University?

This is a problem that many of us face a few times in our life:

- First, when we decide to attend college;
- Again, when we consider further education;
- Finally, when we have to put our own kids through college.

Many university students change majors sometime during their four-year program. They often lose up to a year due to a poor career choice in the first place.

In the previous survey that we conducted, we found that, three months before graduation, only 42% of high school seniors had identified at least three universities they would apply to.

All too often parents and children struggle though these

Career Guidance— Which University?

- Location/distance
- Location/weather
- City, small town, etc.
- Fame – primary subject
- Availability of secondary subject
- Cost of tuition
- Cost of living
- Scholarships
- Name recognition
- Duration of course
- Teacher/student ratio
- Sports fame
- Extracurricular activities
- Religious affiliations
- Academic demands
- Accommodations
- Quality of teaching
- Diversity of student body

decisions. During my tenure as a university professor, I helped dozens of confused young men and women decide on a career.

I suggest you identify the type of profession that interests you before seeking a college. Having done that, you can use some of the criteria shown in the box to make your decision. Of course, you may add any additional criteria that may apply in your case.

Even if you do not have sufficient information on the candidates (universities), you can select the *obligatory* criteria and assign weights.

Eight

Selecting a School

Selecting a School
- Public or private
- Day or boarding
- City or rural
- Cost
- Reputation
- Distance from home
- Cultural diversity
- Facilities
- Sports program
- Music/art program
- Religious affiliation
- Social environment
- Special programs
- Successful alumni
- Educational philosophy
- Teaches the fundamentals
- Enjoyable school
- Develops creativity
- Develops good work habits
- Safety & security
- Quality of teachers
- Discipline
- Intellectually challenging
- School management

Most families have to make a decision on a school for their kids. If you plan to send them to a public school, there is not much of a choice. However, if you plan to use a private school or a pre-school, *XpertUS* will come in handy.

Use some of the criteria shown in the box, add your own, and use the 7-step method we discussed.

Consider, for example, *public* vs. *private*. This criterion remains obligatory, unless the evaluator decides that it be a prerequisite. The same holds true for *Day* or *Boarding, City* or *Rural,* etc.

Nine

Deciding on a Small Business

Recently Mark and Tina Watson asked me to assist them in their decision to acquire a business. I will discuss this case using the 7-step process.

STEP 1: Study the problem, and clearly define your objective

It was clear from the out-set that the objective was not sufficiently specific. Therefore, I asked them to expand on their objective. We confirmed that developing a business from grass roots was not an option. After several gyrations, we restated the objective — *to acquire a business as a part-time venture.*

Original Criteria List

1. Price**
2. Capital outlay**
3. Additional borrowing requirements
4. Owner financing
5. Owner's time commitment**
6. Number of employees required
7. Dependence on employee trust
8. Immediate competitive risks
9. Future competitive risks
10. Risk – due to policy changes
11. Profitability – Return on Investment
12. Resale potential in 3-5 years
13. Comfort level (safety, mental pressure, etc.)
14. Growth potential
15. Verifiable accounts*
16. Ability to monitor business*

** Absolute Prerequisites
* Limiting prerequisites

STEP 2: Write down all the criteria and define the prerequisites, including the limiting conditions

We listed every criterion that came to mind, but we also limited our criteria to the candidates the client had specified (see #4). We had an accountant review the list. Subsequently, we analyzed the list of criteria and extracted the prerequisites.

STEP 3: Extract *obligatory* criteria

Since we had only thirteen criteria, there was no need to do a criteria segregation. Three were absolute prerequisites.

STEP 4: Select all available candidates (options) that meet all prerequisites

After further discussions, I realized that they had the following candidates in mind:

- A liquor store
- A daycare center
- An automotive repair service

Note that this is a case where we had the candidates defined *a priori*. Thus we did not have to go through a session on creative thinking to generate candidates.

STEP 5: Gather information on candidates; also any new criteria

This was the client's responsibility. I cannot present the details here due to a confidentiality agreement.

STEP 6: Assign weights to the *obligatory* criteria

We ran *XpertUS* and assigned weights.

STEP 7: Rank candidates

Finally, we used *XpertUS* to rank the candidates. The results were as follows:

1. Automotive Repair Shop — 49.30%
2. Daycare Center — 35.40%
3. Liquor Store — 15.30%

(Note: you can always do steps 6 and 7 simultaneously.)

Ten

Small Business Advertising Campaign

Many small businesses are often in a quandary as to how to advertise. Here are some guidelines that might be helpful.

STEP 1: Study the problem and clearly define your objective

This is a very difficult step. All one really knows is that one should advertise. We can use a criteria evaluation to identify the best approach.

Criteria for Advertising Campaign

- Budgetary constraints
- Duration of campaign
- Advertising season
- Advertising frequency
- Resources to handle inquiries
- Distribution network
- Market: local, statewide, national
- Market: age group
- Market: lifestyle
- Market: buying habits
- Market: financial worth
- Market: gender (male/female)

STEP 2: Write down all the criteria and define the prerequisites, including the limiting conditions

I have provided a few criteria; you can add your own. Also set your limiting conditions.

STEP 3: Extract *obligatory* criteria

Since we have only a few criteria, there is no need to do a criteria segregation.

STEP 4: Select all available candidates (options) that meet all prerequisites

I have provided a list of typical candidates.

STEP 5: Gather information on candidates; also add any new criteria

This requires work on your part.

STEP 6: Assign weights to the *obligatory* criteria

Run *XpertUS* and assign weights.

STEP 7: Rank candidates

Finally, run *XpertUS* to rank the candidates.

(Note: you can always do steps 6 and 7 simultaneously.)

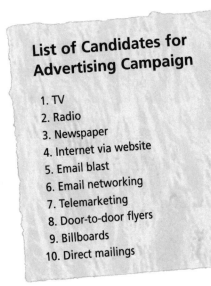

List of Candidates for Advertising Campaign

1. TV
2. Radio
3. Newspaper
4. Internet via website
5. Email blast
6. Email networking
7. Telemarketing
8. Door-to-door flyers
9. Billboards
10. Direct mailings

Part Four

Appendices
(For Further Reading)

1. Selecting a Good Decision-Making Tool

2. Case Study: Downing of a Libyan Airliner

3. Brainstorming

4. *XpertUS*—Virtues and Reliability

5. The Proposal

6. A Guide to Negotiating

7. Job Categories—U.S. Department of Labor

8. Test Your Decision-Making Prowess—
   Some Examples

9. Answers to Problems

Selecting a Good Decision-Making Tool

Throughout this book I have discussed factors that impact decision-making. Following is a brief summary of the requirements of a good decision-making tool:

GUIDES THE DECISION-MAKER

Without a doubt, the most important feature of a good decision-making tool is that it provides a reliable, time-consistent ranking process; it should not make the decision for the user, but guide him/her to the best decision.

MINIMIZES SUBJECTIVITY

Subjectivity is the *Achilles heel* of decision-making, and I have stressed its negative impact throughout this book. While there is no way to eliminate subjectivity totally, any good tool should attempt to minimize subjective influences.

HELPS WITH CRITERIA SELECTION

When you start identifying criteria, it is easy to come up with every conceivable criterion, however insignificant. A good decision-making tool should allow the user to study the significance of the various criteria and should help him/her identify the most relevant ones. Based on our studies, we recommend limiting the number of criteria to between eight and twelve.

Helps weight criteria

In addition to assisting in identifying the most relevant criteria, a good decision-making tool should guide the user in assigning weights to each criterion in a manner that truly reflects the user's desires and expectations. A tool that does not provide this is of little value.

Accepts inconsistencies

Inconsistency is a natural human trait. In any comparative evaluation, it is highly probable that we might conclude that A > B, B > C, C > D, and suddenly say that D > A. Though this might be obvious when stated now, it is not as obvious when viewed separately. Any tool capable of monitoring such inconsistencies is exceptionally valuable.

Determines if the decision is valid / reliable

A good decision-making tool should confirm the validity of the final decision. Remember, *garbage in, garbage out.* What use is a final ranking if we have a low level of confidence in it?

Avoids the need for group comparisons

If the model is provided judgments based on *group comparisons,* you will reach a highly subjective, sub-optimal decision regardless of how good your decision-making model is. In addition to being highly subjective, *group comparison* is not consistent.

Provides transparency

The decision-making process should be transparent, visible, overt, and auditable. Transparency adds credibility to the final decision. What use is a decision if the rest of the world does not have faith in the process used to arrive at the decision?

Rankings should be reliable and consistent

A good decision-making tool should be tested against known *quantitative* tests to confirm reliability. Additionally the results should be consistent. If you were to repeat the same exercise in three months, you should reach the same conclusion unless conditions have changed.

ALLOWS THE USER TO CONDUCT SENSITIVITY STUDIES

Sensitivity studies are a necessary part of any decision-making process. After you run the first analysis, you must study the impact of the various criteria. A good tool allows you to conduct such studies with minimum effort.

CONSOLIDATES MULTI-DECISIONS

Most decisions are made by a team or by individuals within a team; thus, it is necessary to consolidate the individual results to arrive at a final decision. A good decision-making tool should provide for such consolidation.

PEER EVALUATIONS

Provides for members of a team to rank themselves.

OTHER FEATURES

Multi-lingual; multi-user; user-friendly; affordable; does not require formal training or prior experience.

—◁▯◁▯▷—

The *XpertUS* decision-maker was developed to meet all of the above requirements.

Case Study:
Downing of a Libyan Airliner
by Israeli Fighter Jets

THE INCIDENT (Situation Assessment):

On February 21, 1973, a Libyan plane flying from Benghazi, Libya to Cairo, Egypt, strayed, and entered the airspace over the Israeli-occupied Sinai Peninsula. Israeli radar detected the hostile intrusion of a plane from an Arab country (concrete information). Two Israeli F-4 Phantom Fighter Jets were dispatched to intercept the plane.

Everybody was aware of the escalating tensions in the region (context information). Now the decision-makers had to use their experience (expertise) and the information to analyze the situation and decide:

1. Was this an innocent airliner merely off course?

2. Was this a terrorist plane intent on crashing into the Israeli capital?

SEQUENCE OF EVENTS (Information):

1. The F-4s identified the plane to be a Libyan Boeing 727.

2. The plane was asked to identify itself, but could not be reached by radio.

3. Israelis checked traffic on military communication channels, and found no evidence of this plane.

4. They further checked traffic on civilian airwaves, and again found nothing.

5. F-4 pilots could not see any passengers, since all the window shades were down.

6. One F-4 came within 3 meters of the plane, on the right, and signaled (by hand) to the co-pilot to land.

7. The F-4 reported that the co-pilot looked straight at the F-4 pilot, and lowered the undercarriage, indicating that he understood the commands.

8. However, the plane suddenly turned back as if heading home, to escape.

9. Despite warning shots, the plane continued.

10. After conferring with his superiors, General Hod ordered the F-4 pilots to force the plane to land—by shooting at its wingtips.

11. Then one F-4 shot at the wings, and forced the plane to crash-land, safely.

12. Unfortunately, even though the plane landed safely, it hit a sand dune and exploded. All but one of the 123 passengers and crew died.

CONTEXT:

1. The presence of the airliner was particularly alarming.

2. Israeli intelligence had warned about a possible terrorist attack using a hijacked plane.

3. General Hod was an experienced war veteran who had been involved in the Six-day War.

4. This plane had entered Egyptian airspace, and Egyptian Air Defenses had not reacted.

5. A few months earlier, an Ethiopian airliner that strayed into Egyptian airspace was shot down.

6. Several other planes had received warning shots, when they penetrated free-fire airspaces marked on maps that indicated they would be shot down without warning.

7. Pilots are very familiar with free-fire zones, and stay far away from them.

GENERAL HOD'S TESTIMONY (Expert Analysis):

1. We were aware of a terrorist plan to hijack a plane, and threaten to explode it, to force Israel to release prisoners.

2. The plane was spotted in an area where there had been engagements with Egyptian fighter planes.

3. Radar warning was "hostile intrusion" with no specifics about the type of plane.

4. The plane was flying at jet speeds. Civilian airliners do fly at these speeds, but only on long-range flights.

5. The plane was over very sensitive Egyptian airspace, and the Egyptians had not responded.

6. The plane appeared to have avoided Israeli ground-to-air missile bases, where it would have been shot down automatically.

7. Given that civilian captains have the safety of their passengers foremost in their mind, it was unthinkable that he would risk lives.

8. We tried to establish communications with Cairo on all available channels, but failed.

9. We assumed that the captain would have seen the Star of David painted on the F-4s, and could see the airfield where he was ordered to land.

10. The pilot released the undercarriage, and then retracted it.

11. The plane circled the airfield, as if it was trying to get a better approach, and then took off.

12. With every event, we became more convinced that this was a hijacked plane.

13. When the F-4s fired, the pilot should have seen the tracer bullets; yet he continued westwards, headed back home.

14. Even after we shot at the wingtips, the Libyans remained indifferent.

15. Why were all the shades drawn? Some may be down; but not all—unless someone ordered all shades be drawn.

16. All this happened at lightning speed.

17. We felt compelled to force-land it, to find out why it was so obstinate. We did not want this apparent "terrorist" plane to escape.

18. I passed all this information to General Elazar (chief of Israeli Defense Forces), who agreed with my assessment of the situation.

THE REST OF THE STORY:
(From subsequent investigation and black box recordings)

1. The crew consisted of a French captain and a flight engineer communicating in French, and a Libyan co-pilot who did not speak French. The French had completely ignored the Libyan co-pilot.

2. They had been drinking wine, and were 70 miles off course; but hadn't a clue as to their whereabouts.

3. They mistakenly identified the F-4s as MIGs.

4. When the co-pilot asked the French captain to land, he reassured him, saying that these were Egyptian MIGs, and they were headed to Cairo.

5. The F-4s were communicating with the Libyan co-pilot, and the Frenchmen ignored him completely.

6. Because Egypt and Libya have excellent relations, the French captain was certain that the Egyptians would never shoot down a Libyan civilian plane.

7. Finally, when what they thought were the MIGs started to shoot, they thought the fighter pilots had gone berserk, and decided to crash-land.

8. Because Cairo had a military airport to the east and a civilian airport to the west, the captain had thought they were over Egypt; that he had blundered and was headed to the military airport (hence the MIGs). So, he changed directions and headed west.

9. Gen. Hod missed a cue that the plane was approached on the *right* side, where the co-pilot was.

FAILED DECISION

Information-providing instruments did not know of the situation surrounding this information (e.g., wine-drinking pilots, language barriers, etc.), yet the information was presented to General Hod as highly reliable.

With every passing moment, the information was appearing to be more reliable, possibly because the stakes were very high, and time was critical.

What was the primary objective of the Israeli Defense Forces? Guaranteeing the security of the Israeli nation.

However, as the situation unraveled, with each action they were more convinced that this was a terrorist threat, and General Hod lost sight of his primary objective. He was now hell-bent on finding out why this rogue plane had attempted to enter Israeli-occupied airspace. This led to his decision to force the airliner to land.

Appendix Three

Brainstorming

Outline of the Brainstorming Process

Identify and clearly define the Objective.

Select the three key people: The *expert*, the *recorder*, and the *facilitator*.

Invite about twenty participants. Who you invite depends on the objective. If it is a highly technical issue, you need to invite people with adequate knowledge and education in the area under discussion. However, in cases that are *strategic* in nature, you must invite people from as many diverse groups as possible. They must have different levels of education and experience.

THE EXPERT

The first step in a brainstorming session is the PAS/PAU phase.

PAS — Problem as Stated
PAU — Problem as Understood

Very often this is tied to a poor statement of the problem. Therefore the expert should ensure that everybody understands what is expected of him/her. Explain the problem in lay terms that everyone can understand. Remember, many of the participants are probably not familiar with the subject matter, so the expert must give them adequate time to ask questions, but does not entertain ideas or solutions.

The *expert* does not participate in the session, except as an observer. In fact, it is preferable for the expert to leave the room after making his/her presentation, as the participants might find his/her presence intimidating.

THE RECORDER

Records the suggestions in an orderly manner for subsequent analysis. These notes will be required for projection or display later on.

THE FACILITATOR

1. Ensures that the group stays on course.
2. Ensures that the *expert* is confined to his/her role.
3. Ensures that the *recorder* is confined to recording suggestions.
4. Keeps an up-beat attitude and creates a participative mood.
5. Ensures that no one is left behind due to inhibitions.
6. Does not let anyone dominate.
7. Frequently invites everyone to participate.
8. Explains the "warm-up" example.
9. Makes the event fun and playful—gets the participants to relax.
10. Imposes time limits.
11. Does not try to direct or influence the process except as discussed above.

—⸎—

The Process

STEP 1 – Conduct

- Explain the code of conduct and the ground rules (as stated above).
- Stress that no one is to comment critically or otherwise, on suggestions.
- Stress that no idea is wrong, bad, or inappropriate.

STEP 2 – Warm-up

- Start the process with the warm-up example. For this exercise the "warm-up" example is: "What are the possible uses for a paper-clip?" Other examples could be a toothpick, or a broom.
- Limit the warm-up example to twenty minutes.

- Stress that the participants must shoot for "quantity" of ideas, rather than "quality."
- Once all the suggestions are listed, take a ten-minute break.

STEP 3 – Introduce expert and present problem

- Introduce the *expert* and let him/her explain the problem. Use the guidelines provided on P-152.

STEP 4 – Problem

- Have the group brainstorm the actual problem.
- Impose a twenty-minute time limit.

STEP 5 – Compile suggestions

- Once the mission is complete, take a fifteen-minute break.
- During this break, select a couple of participants (or secretaries) to sort through the suggestions and put them in a structured format. Do not eliminate any option unless it is a duplicate.

STEP 6 – Review suggestions

- Regroup the team, this time including the *expert*. Review the suggestions to determine if they are plausible and of value. This is a delicate situation. The *expert* will try to undermine ideas from newcomers. I have come across *negative* thinkers in every situation. These people insist that anything new is unworkable. It is the job of the facilitator to curb these *killers of creativity*.

STEP 7 – Conclusion

- Once the team has agreed on a list of possible solutions, the facilitator thanks the participants and concludes the brainstorming session.

STEP 8 – Further analysis

- The suggestions are then submitted to management for further analysis.

Facilities

Arrange the seats with the names of the participants clearly marked; if at all possible keep *buddies* apart.

Ensure that there is adequate space. Do not crowd a large group into a small room. Participants must feel relaxed and have comfortable seats.

Cell phones, pagers, etc., must be switched off; even in a "meeting" mode they are a source of distraction.

If possible, serve some refreshments before the meeting to allow the participants to get to know each other.

Brainstorming sessions are not limited to the business world. Don't be bashful. If you have a personal problem, call up a few friends and conduct a brainstorming session.

Limitations

It is difficult to say if creativity is an inborn talent or if we are molded into being creative. This we leave to the psychologists. However, it is interesting to note that there seems to be a general relationship between professions and how decisions are made. Here are some examples.

- **The Train Driver**

  He has an assigned job, with a route and a schedule provided. He is required to comply with instructions issued to him and is not trained to be creative. Basically, he does not get paid to think about how to improve service or increase revenue, and he does not decide on new routes. When he is faced with a decision-making situation, he follows set guidelines.

- **The Physician**

  He is a problem-solver; he keeps an eye on the human body and reacts to problems. The doctor-type does not change the existing system. He is content if the system works.

- ## The Farmer

  The farmer is always trying to maximize yield. Though he strives to do better, his creativity is tied to incremental improvements. He cannot think out-of-box. He will try to maximize but not optimize.

- ## The Attorney

  The attorney does not try to improve the system with new ideas. Rather, he tries to use the system to beat the system for the benefit of his client. He will show that, under certain scenarios, a perceived problem is not really a problem. His decisions will always revolve around interpretations.

- ## The Advertiser

  People who create advertisements are the most courageous of all. They venture into unknown territory and cast their nets. They make decisions that determine the success or failure of an enterprise. This sort of person is a real asset in brainstorming, since he/she is the one who generates visionary ideas on a daily basis.

- ## The Comedian

  He/she is the creative type. He/she sees the world as a place where chaos thrives, and is constantly looking for odd patterns and behaviors. The comedian's lighthearted approach helps break down inhibitions, which is vital to a successful brainstorming session.

Case Study: Pot-holes in Bolivia

The owner of a road-repair company in Bolivia needed to generate more business. Even though many roads in the country were in very poor

Pot-holes

1. Increase in tire imports—resulting from excessive wear and tear.

2. Cost of spare parts and maintenance—vehicles take a heavy toll.

3. Productive time lost—due to commuters driving very slowly, negotiating pot-holes, and also seeking alternate routes.

4. Increased fuel consumption.

5. Added pollution of the environment.

condition, he had not been able to convince the authorities to spend money to improve road conditions. As a consultant on this project, I recommended that the benefits of road repairs be quantified considering foreign-exchange losses and environmental issues (See Box).

XpertUS —
Virtues and Reliability

XpertUS was developed to incorporate all the requirements of a good decision-making tool. Additionally, *XpertUS* offers several other benefits.

Virtues

— Ranks criteria and candidates using pairwise comparison

I discussed the merits of pairwise comparison and also provided several examples to back these claims. Pairwise comparison provides reliable decisions, but more importantly, decisions that are consistent over time.

— An excellent training tool

The decision-making technique presented within *XpertUS* is ideal for evolving professionals. With frequent use of *XpertUS* and the *Aim-Preset* technique, they will develop the art and skill of decision-making.

— Allows the user to conduct sensitivity studies

Sensitivity studies are a necessary part of any decision-making process. After you run the first analysis, you must study the impact of the various criteria. A good tool allows you to conduct such studies with minimum effort.

— Allows consolidation and peer evaluation

These two features are extremely valuable—as many decisions are conducted in a team environment.

— Allows delegation of decision-making

Once younger managers are comfortable with using *XpertUS*, senior management can confidently delegate decision-making responsibilities. This will allow senior management to concentrate on more significant issues.

— Internet-based

XpertUS is the only pay-per-use decision-making tool that is accessible worldwide via the Internet. Users do not have to purchase a high-priced software package; payment is based on usage.

— Multi-lingual

XpertUS is available in several languages.

Reliability

Two tests are presented to confirm the reliability of *XpertUS*.

— The "Inverse Square Law of Light" (Physics)

This law states that, *the intensity of light at a given point is inversely proportional to the square of the distance of that point from the light source.* Can *XpertUS* prove this law?

Four white sheets of paper were positioned at distances of 10, 16, 24 and 36 feet from a light source. Students were asked to compare the intensity of light falling on each sheet of paper as compared to the others. This information was fed to *XpertUS*, which showed the intensity levels to be:

61.40   23.90   10.30   4.50

Now, if we were to take the distances 10, 16, 24 and 36 feet, square them and take their reciprocals, we get 0.0100, 0.0039, 0.0017, and 0.0007. If we normalize this we have:

60.92   23.80   10.58   4.70

This compares extremely well with the *XpertUS* results. The total deviation is 1.06%. By any standards, this is well within acceptable limits of accuracy!

Imagine you are looking at these four sheets of paper and trying to guess the brightness ratios. This is a near-impossible task; yet with *XpertUS,* people were able to arrive at a highly reliable conclusion!

The Power of *XpertUS*

I conducted an interesting series of experiments to prove the superior value of *XpertUS*. There were three objectives.

OBJECTIVE I: As the number of candidates increases, does decision-making become more difficult?

I asked five individuals to look at pictures of seven ladies.

I started with two pictures (candidates) and asked the group to use all three evaluation methods (*distribution, scaling,* and *XpertUS)* to rank the candidates. Then I increased the number to four candidates and asked them to repeat the process. Finally, we repeated the evaluations with all seven candidates.

Now imagine doing this experiment. Would you not agree that comparing

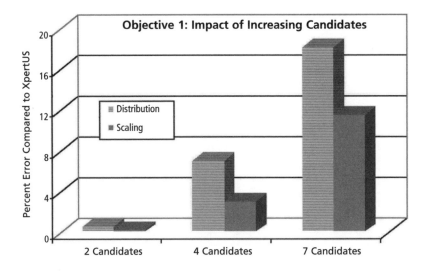

a pair is much easier than comparing a group and also likely to be more consistent?

We used the *XpertUS* evaluation as our reference and observed that the deviation (errors) of the rankings determined by the other two methods increased significantly as the number of candidates increased. Thus, a tool such as *XpertUS* is invaluable, especially when you have many candidates.

OBJECTIVE 2: Is the pairwise technique superior to other techniques?

- On the first day, I asked the participants to distribute one hundred points among all of the contestants to reflect their facial beauty.
- The next day, I asked them to assign points on a scale of 1-10.
- On the third day, I asked them to rank the contestants using *XpertUS*.

The graph shows the results. Of course, because of the simplicity of the pairwise technique, *XpertUS* provides the most reliable ranking.

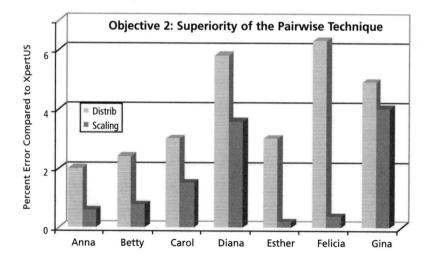

OBJECTIVE 3: How consistent are the results provided by *XpertUS*?

My hypothesis was that subjective decisions are not consistent over time. Since *XpertUS* minimizes subjectivity, it follows that the *XpertUS* technique is superior to the other two techniques.

We repeated the tests thirty, sixty, and ninety days later. The evidence indicated conclusively that the *XpertUS* technique is consistent over time (see graph).

This result is to be expected because the judgment of the average person when comparing two items is far more consistent than judgments comparing multiple items.

The human mind is far more capable of comparing two items than a group of items. Through experimental testing, it was proven conclusively that the pairwise comparison technique is significantly superior to the group comparison technique:

A: When group size increases

B: With the passage of time.

XpertUS is Reliable and Consistent!

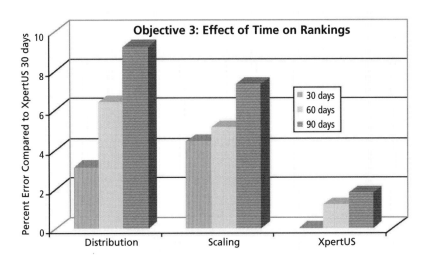

Appendix Five

The Proposal

Some time ago, I assisted a friend who wanted to add an extension (a game room with an attached patio) to his home. After some initial discussions, I sat down and wrote out the specifications for the job. In the bid request, I asked the potential bidders to itemize their quotes so we could eliminate any work that we would do ourselves.

I sent the specifications to eight contractors, giving them one week to submit written quotes. Once I received the bids, I built my criteria list.

Following a cursory review, I realized that prices had been greatly inflated. I had to find a way to negotiate a better price. I rejected the most expensive one, since it was nearly 15% above the next highest bid. Additionally, I rejected the lowest bidder since he came in with a ridiculously low figure that made me doubt his understanding of our requirements. I summarized the rest of the bids, and ranked them using *XpertUS*.

I called the wining bidder, and we sat down and negotiated a mutually acceptable agreement. In these types of dealings, you must always remember the collaborative or win-win approach to negotiating. You do not want to win by slamming your opponent to the ground. He/she must feel good at the end; otherwise you will be left with shabby workmanship or cheap material, which you may not spot before payment.

1. I made him feel that his proposal had been subjected to a very thorough evaluation and that he had won on merit. It was important to make him feel good. *(Make your opponent feel good)*

2. I showed him my evaluation (without the pricing information) to let him know that I did my work in a very professional manner. *(Gain respect)*

3. We started talking about his workload and soon I realized that he wanted this job badly. *(Pick up cues during the negotiation)*

4. Before we entered into a deeper discussion, I negotiated a price reduction of 10% on each item. This was not very difficult. I knew that he had increased prices to allow for negotiations. *(Trim the fat)*

5. Then, I wrote the new reduced prices on the bid document so that we had a written reference of our agreements. *(Document points of agreement)*

6. I excluded areas that we thought we could do ourselves, but did not add up the numbers. If he were to see the new total, he would feel that he had come down significantly from his original total price. I did not want him to be aware of my strategy. *(Do not disclose strategy)*

7. I told him, "Jack, I am now happy with the pricing and am confident that you can do the work." I worked on building his ego. I could see the glee in his eyes. *(Re-emphasize self-esteem)*

8. Finally, I offered my payment plan: 10% on startup; another 40% on completion; 25%—30 days after completion; and the final 25% —30 days later. He said I had not told him about the payment plan. I said he had not asked, and that I thought he was able to fund his projects; but maybe I was mistaken. My justification was—warranty. We haggled on this one. He thought he had the contract, and suddenly he was about to lose it. He said he would have to "factor" my invoice. (Factoring is a method of financing, where an investor would buy a short-term receivable account at about 80-90 cents on the dollar). I pointed out that if he were a supplier to any major retailer, payments would be 100% in 60 days—mine was significantly better. He was vehemently opposed to this. *(Exit strategy)*

9. Then I introduced an incentive; I said I would pay the balance (50%) on completion—if he would drop the price by 5%. Additionally, I would pay by check instead of by credit card, thereby saving him a further 2%. We finally settled for a 3% price reduction. *(Win–win closure)*

Appendix Six

A Guide to Negotiating: Useful Negotiating Tips!

1. Conduct negotiations in a manner that conforms to legal, ethical, and moral standards.

2. Always stay focused on your objective. Be aware of the consequences of not reaching an agreement.

3. Remember the PI Rule: Before you start negotiating, establish reference values; identify *positions* and *interests*. Separate *people* from *issues*.

4. Gather as much information as you can on the subject and on your opponent.

5. Never be the first to offer a compromise or split the difference. The person who first makes an offer has weakened his/her position. It signifies that this person is willing to give up a little more. Keep hinting at a possible compromise, but let your opponent be the originator. After your opponent offers a significant concession, you must always reciprocate.

6. Listen carefully to the spoken word. When a person says, "In my humble opinion", he is not being humble at all. Pay close attention to the opponent's choice of words, especially the adjectives and adverbs, as this will most certainly provide clues to his/her direction and intentions.

7. Always agree initially; this diffuses the competitive spirit. One day Lady Astor told Winston Churchill: "You are disgusting; you are so drunk". Churchill told her: "Lady Astor, you are so right! I am drunk! But you are ugly. In the morning I shall be sober. . . ."

8. Leverage not only your strengths, but also the strengths and weaknesses of your opponent. Every situation gives you some leverage, and you need to creatively seek and identify these elements. Play your winners judiciously.

9. Revert to a "higher authority". Always have a "phantom" higher authority, or better still, a committee, to check back with.

10. Never underestimate your opponents. It is better to let them underestimate you and drop their guard. Do not let your opponents think that they are dealing with a smart cookie. You will only encourage them to better prepare themselves. Dumb is smarter: sophistication breeds competition. However, you need them to know that they are dealing with a professional.

11. Whether you are buying or selling, you should have a walk-away or a reconsideration limit. Set it before you enter the discussion.

12. Write it down! Recognize the power of the written word. Wherever possible use *quantitative* arguments over *qualitative* statements. In real estate dealings counter-offers are given in writing. Use unit values: Cost per passenger mile; cost per person per hour.

13. Always empathize with your opponent's position.

14. Subtly let your opponents know that they cannot get a better deal from your boss or from someone else. Your opponents must be able to respect you, and recognize that you are their best option.

15. Establish credibility. Your opponent should realize that you are a person of your word, and trust that you will deliver on any agreement.

16. Be cognizant of the influence of culture and religion. This is vital to your success.

17. Position the opponent to win. Start with some ludicrous demands (as in union negotiations) so that your opponent will feel he has won. Never say, *yes* to the first offer. The other person needs to feel that they *won* this deal. Negotiate to let them feel good. Additionally, this will let you trade off for something that really matters.

18. Be fair and reasonable. An opponent will not feel bad at conceding if he/she feels that you have acted "fairly".

19. Start with a reasonable concession; then reduce the size of future concessions.

20. Always keep in mind the differences in personality styles.

21. Be engaging: try to break down suspicions and barriers.

22. Do not stress or emphasize your opponent's mistakes or factual errors to hurt his ego unless you are certain that it would serve your interests.

23. Be judicious in deciding when to set the direction and tempo of the negotiation: when it is appropriate to lead and when to follow.

24. Manage the situation cautiously. There is a fine balance between gaining an advantage and compromising.

25. Be authoritative, but not arrogant. You must be likeable. Your posture, style, and substance should not be obnoxious or threatening.

TACTICS

1. Association—Name Dropping: "Your HR Director, Bill, mentioned this at our dinner."

2. Blanketing: "Everyone is offering some sort of concession."

3. Resource Limit: "You have a product of value; but we are limited on resources."

4. Moral Appeal: "You know we need this. I am sure you can help us get it."

5. Flinch—React in amazement: "That much?"

6. If/Then—Conditional Trade: "I will give this if you are willing to give ..."

7. Higher Authority: "I really have to get this approved by my manager."

8. Missing Man: "Our legal expert is out of the office."

9. Precedent: "This is how we have always done this."

10. Trial Balloon: "Well, for the sake of discussion ..."

11. Competition: "If we cannot agree, we can always go out for bids again."

12. Ultimatum: "This is my final offer. We have to make a decision today."

13. Nibbling: Keep asking for a little more, each time. "I am inclined to agree since you are paying for the extended warranty."

14. Withdrawal Gesture: "I get the feeling that there is no point in continuing this discussion."

15. Good Guy/Bad Guy: "You do not want to face my boss on this one. He will be more demanding."

16. Reversal—Taking back your offer: "I've given you too many concessions, I will have to go back to our original "limited" warranty."

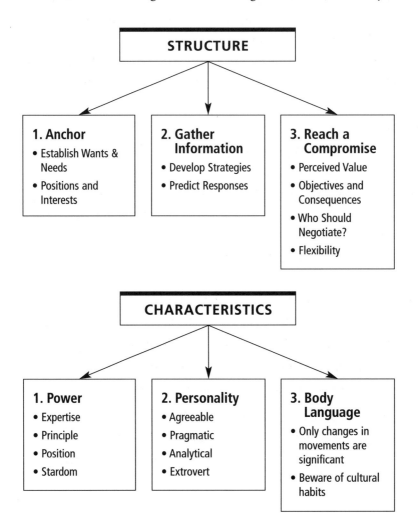

Job Categories — U.S. Department of Labor

T he U.S. Dept. of Labor has grouped all professions and job titles (in excess of 20,000) into 19 families. This is a good starting point for career planning for high-school students.

1. Managerial and Management-related Occupations

2. Engineers, Surveyors and Architects

3. Natural, Computer and Mathematical Scientists

4. Lawyers, Social Scientists, Social Welfare Workers, and Religious Workers

5. Teachers, Librarians and Counselors

6. Health Diagnosing and Treatment Practitioners

7. Registered Nurses, Pharmacists, Dietitians, Therapists, and Physicians' Assistants

8. Health Technologists and Technicians

9. Writers, Artists, and Entertainers

10. Non-health related Technologists and Technicians

11. Marketing and Sales Occupations

12. Administrative Support Occupations, including Clerical

13. Service Occupations

14. Agriculture, Forestry, Fishing and Related Occupations

15. Mechanics, Installers and Repairmen

16. Construction Trades and Extractive Occupations

17. Production Occupations

18. Transportation and Material Moving Occupations

19. Handlers, Equipment Cleaners, Helpers, and Laborers

Test Your Decision-Making Prowess —Some Examples

There is little purpose in reading this book unless you recognize you can benefit from improved techniques.

Here are a few examples to help determine how good you are at making decisions. This simple reality-check will help put *XpertUS* in its proper perspective; this is a self-help book designed to help you! These are not trick problems, and do not require the use of mathematics.

I will start with simple problems involving lateral thinking and follow them with more difficult decision-making problems. The answers are provided in Appendix 9.

LATERAL THINKING

TEST #1: The Not-So-Identical Coins (Power of Reasoning)

You are given eight identical looking coins and a *twin-pan* weighing scale; one coin is slightly heavier than the rest.

QUESTION: How would you identify the heavier coin using the scales only twice?

TEST #2: The *Mysterious* Light-Switch (Lateral Thinking)

Consider two adjacent rooms. There are three light-switches in one room, one of which operates a table lamp in the adjacent room.

QUESTION: Can you determine which switch would turn on the light? You have only one opportunity to go to the adjacent room to check whether the light is on.

TEST #3: The Elevator Problem[14]

Tenants of a very tall office building in New York were complaining about delays associated with the elevators. Various consultants recommended operating at higher speeds, shortening the doors' opening and closing times, stopping at alternate floors, and using designated elevator banks to serve only a given set of floors, etc. At the end of the day, none of these stopped the complaints. Finally, Dr. De Bono was invited to address the problem.

QUESTION: How would you solve this problem?

TEST #4: The Dumb Dog[14]

Dr. De Bono presented this problem to a group of CEOs.

A man buys a watchdog. It turns out that the dog does not bark. What should the man do?

He received the following suggestions:
1. Buy a barking dog.
2. Train the dog to press an alarm.
3. Take it back, complain, and try to trade it in—report the matter to the Consumer Protection Agency.
4. Train it to fetch its handler.
5. Switch on a photoelectric beam so that when he leaves his kennel, an alarm is triggered.

6. Have a sensing alarm strapped to the dog's back, which will trigger the device and activate an alarm.
7. Train the dog to switch on a tape-recording of a dog barking.
8. Find out why he does not bark and put the matter right.
9. Install burglar alarms as well.

QUESTION: What would you recommend?

TEST #5: Linda's Profession

Several researchers tried to design a problem that defines *logic*. Birnbaum, Davidson, Shafir, and Wolford[15] discussed the following problem:

Linda is 31 years old, single, bright, and outspoken. She majored in philosophy. As a student, she was deeply concerned with issues of discrimination and social justice and also participated in anti-nuclear demonstrations.

A – Is an elementary school teacher.

B – Works in a bookstore and takes Yoga classes.

C – Is active in the feminist movement.

D – Is a psychiatric social worker.

E – Is a member of the League of Women Voters.

F – Is a bank teller.

G – Is an insurance sales person.

H – Is a bank teller and is active in the feminist movement.

What is Linda's most likely profession (see box)?
(Rank from 1 – 8; 1 = least likely, 8 = most likely)

QUESTION: If you had to select between F & H, which would seem more likely?

TEST #6A: Cards Hypothesis

Each of the cards below has a number on one side and a letter on the other side. You can only see the sides shown below.

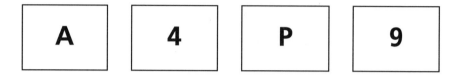

Rule: A card with a *vowel* should have an *even* number on the back.

QUESTION: Which cards should we turn (as a minimum) to confirm the rule?

TEST #6B: Drinking Problem Hypothesis

Now consider a more real-life problem: A police officer confronts four persons. Each card represents the person's action on one side and the person's age on the other. You can only see the sides shown below.

Rule: If a person is consuming alcohol, then the person must be over 19 years.

QUESTION: Which cards should the officer turn over (as a minimum) to determine who is violating the rule?

Test #7: The Killer-Bee Problem (Use the Aim-Preset Technique)

The U.S. has been grappling with the problem of South American killer-bees reaching its borders. Use the Aim-Preset technique to identify potential solutions to this problem.

Test #8: The Nomad With The Gold Rod

A nomad was lost in the desert. All he had was a 7-kg gold rod and a saw. Each kilo was marked clearly on the rod. He was almost at his wit's end when he saw a man riding a camel in front of him. "Could you please help me get to the nearest city?" asked the nomad.

"What is it that you're carrying?" asked the rider.

"It's a 7-kg gold rod," answered the nomad.

"I'll tell you what we do," said the rider. "The nearest city is exactly 70 km away, so pay me 1 kg. of gold now, and then pay me 1 kg. every 10 km until we reach the city."

"But my saw can cut the rod only twice," said the nomad. "Perhaps you can accept three payments instead of seven?" he continued.

"No," replied the rider. "I want 1 kg. now and 1 kg. every 10 km. Seven equal payments of 1 kg. or the deal's off".

Eventually, the rider helped the nomad to get to the city, on the camel. How did the nomad pay for the service?

Test #9: The Defective Vending Machine

There are 10 vending machines that dispense candy bars, each weighing 10 grams. However, one machine dispenses candy bars that are 9 grams in weight. Using a digital weighing machine, find the defective candy machine, with only one weighing. You may take as many candy bars as you like from any machine.

DECISION-MAKING

Below are three tests. You need not try all of them, but they will confirm that a powerful tool such as *XpertUS* is invaluable. I invite you to use the following methodology in each case to test your decision-making capabilities:

1. The *distribution* technique:
   (Distribute 100 points among all the items)

2. The *scaling* technique:
   (Assign a number between 1 and 10 to each criterion, with 1 = the least desirable. Now, total all the numbers and then divide each number by the total to normalize the data.)

3. The *XpertUS* technique: (see www.XpertUS.com).

TEST #10: Allocating Spare Time (*XpertUS* Demo-1)

Assume that you have a total of 100 hours per month for these activities. How would you allocate your time among them?

NOTE: Your distribution should reflect how you would like to allocate time, rather than what you are doing at present.

	Distribution %	Scaling 1 – 10	Scaling %	XpertUS %
1. Work at existing job				
2. Work on a second income				
3. Further education				
4. Social contacts/networking				
5. Hobbies/pleasure activities				
6. Charity/community work				
7. Spiritual development				
8. Physical fitness				
9. Family life & support				
Total >>>	100%		100%	100%

TEST #11: Donating Money (*XpertUS* Demo–2)

Imagine you are the administrator of a charity, which has $100,000 to distribute among the following projects:

1. (Education) Jose is the eldest son of a family of seven children, none of whom have ever had academic success. Jose has never seen his father, and his mother is illiterate and an alcoholic. Jose is exceptionally bright and has gained admission to a prestigious university, but needs additional money to be able to attend.

2. (Sight) A blind five-year-old girl has been assured that she would see normally if she were able to come to the USA for an expensive series of operations. In two months, she will be six years old, and beyond this age the surgical procedure would not be effective.

3. (AIDS) In Africa, thousands are dying of AIDS. They need your support to build a treatment center in a remote village. Without this center, many people will die because they are unable to travel the six hundred miles to the nearest existing treatment center.

4. (Earthquake) An earthquake has hit El Salvador and people are forced to drink contaminated water. There is a need to ship and install several water treatment plants.

5. (Environment) The only highway in a small nation is being battered by waves. There is an urgent need to build a barrier. If this is not done, a huge portion of the nation's capitol will go under, with enormous losses.

6. (Iodized salt) In Cambodia, thousands of people are suffering from goiters (enlarged glands in the neck) because the salt they consume does not contain iodine. Funds are required to build a plant to iodize the salt. This will save millions of people from this terrible ailment.

7. (Cancer research) Researchers are fully confident that, with additional funding, they can find a cure for breast cancer. A breakthrough is imminent. Your funds could save millions of women from this dreaded disease.

	Distribution %	Scaling 1 – 10	Scaling %	XpertUS %
1. Education				
2. Sight				
3. AIDS				
4. Earthquake				
5. Environment				
6. Iodized Salt				
7. Cancer Research				
Total >>>	100%		100%	100%

NOTE: Fill in the table above. Remember, your funds help solve these problems; other agencies are also funding these programs. Do not be concerned with how much is required, but give as much as you can.

TEST #12: Criteria for the Homebuyer (*XpertUS* Demo–3)

Imagine that you have decided to buy a house. Consider the list of criteria I have provided below. You need not select all the criteria indicated here, and you may include any additional criteria of your choice. Create a table like the one in the previous example for this problem, and try this using the same techniques as before to assign weights to the criteria.

Typical Criteria For The Homebuyer

Size of house	Cost of utilities	Cost or cost per sq. ft.
Price of house + repairs	Financing	Taxes
Resale potential	Appreciation	Proximity to buses
Age of house	Condition of house	Size of yard
Modern conveniences	Pool	Front appearance
No. of rooms	Floor plan	Proximity to work
Quality of schools	Proximity to schools	Quality of neighborhood
Size of garage	Landscaping	Type of neighbors
Status of location	Likelihood of floods	City or county
Quality of construction	Quality of finish	Availability (time)
	... and others	

When you are ready, sign on to the www.*XpertUS*.com website and use the code that you received from Shanmar Inc. for free access.

Answers to Problems

TEST #1: The Not-So-Identical Coins

Let us identify the coins as—A, B, C, D, E, F, G, H

1. Remove any two from the pile (say G & H). Split the remaining six into two equal groups and place them in the pans (A,B,C in one pan, and D,E,F in the other pan). Weigh them (*first weighing*).

2a. If they weigh the same, then either G or H is the heavier coin. Put G and H on the scales and do a *second weighing,* to determine the heavier coin.

2b. If A+B+C is heavier, then the heavier coin is in that group. Remove A from the pile and compare B and C (*second weighing);* if they are equal, A is the heavier coin, otherwise, B or C is the heavier coin, as seen by the tilt. Obviously, the same process would apply if D+E+F were heavier.

TEST #2: The *Mysterious* Light-Switch

Let us name the switches A, B, C.

Turn on switches A and B, and wait two minutes. Now turn off switch A (leaving B on) and go to the next room.

1. If the light is ON then B is the *hot* switch.
2. If the light is OFF, touch the bulb. If the bulb is hot, A is the *hot* switch; otherwise C is the *hot* switch.

The word *light* appears in the title and several times in the statement of the problem. Naturally everyone focused on *light* and missed a consequence of light energy, which is *heat.*

Lateral thinking requires one to think of direct and consequential impact of various factors. Lateral thinkers focus on redefining the problem to identify the true objective.

TEST #3: Solution to the Elevator Problem

Dr. De Bono realized that the problem was not with the elevators. It was the tenants who were complaining, so he focused on them and how to alleviate their frustrations. He proposed that management install large mirrors in the foyer. Now the tenants focused their attention on looking good rather than looking at the numbers above the elevator doors. The company did not receive any further complaints.

Today, you frequently see TV monitors in elevators and foyers; it was Dr. De Bono who first promoted this idea.

TEST #4: Solution to the Dumb Dog Problem

Dr. De Bono suggested that we try to treat the dog's silence as an opportunity. Erect an illuminated sign that reads:

"Beware of the ferocious, silent watchdog."

The thought of a ferocious, silent dog creeping up on a thief would scare the living daylights out of anyone.

TEST #5: Linda's Profession

This problem was presented to three groups with various degrees of expertise in *statistical analysis*.

The first group did not have any knowledge of statistics; the second group consisted of professionals who had an intermediate knowledge of statistics; all members of the third group were statisticians.

The graph shows that all the groups indicated that Linda was most probably a bank teller and a feminist.

The *conjunction rule* (in statistics) states that the probability of occurrence of two events cannot be greater than the probability of occurrence of its constituent events.

Since this may not sound obvious, consider a more familiar example. How about a psychology class? The number of *psychology* students born in *Texas* (satisfying both conditions) cannot be greater than the number of *psychology* students (satisfying one condition)!

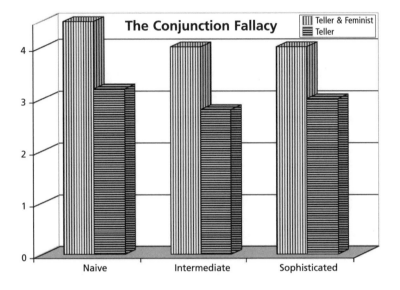

Test #6A: Cards

Answer: A & 9

Why? We do not care if the card "4" or "P" has a dog on the other side. An odd number on the back of "A" or a vowel on the back of number "9" would disprove the rule.

Here is the reason everyone makes a mistake: A card with a vowel having an even number does not necessarily mean that a card with an even number would or should have a vowel.

Test #6B: Drinking Problem

Answer: Drinking Alcohol & Girl of 17 years

Why? The age of the person drinking the Pepsi is immaterial; similarly the boy is over 19 years.

It is interesting to note that in actual tests with groups of students, over seventy percent of the students made the correct decision when dealing with the real-life problem of drinking, yet none picked both correct cards with the abstract problem of numbers.

Beware of erroneous deductive reasoning. Often we make errors in decision-making when we try to prove a hypothesis rather than disprove it.

Test #7: The Killer-Bee Problem (Use the Aim-Preset Technique)

Accept — Treat the people affected with medication.

Isolate — Do not venture into areas where these bees thrive.

Modify — Address the bee genetically—to reduce its impact, or its killer instinct.

Problem —

Replace —

External — Kill the bees—eliminate through a massive program.

Sacrifice — Introduce predators such as bats.

Environment — These bees cannot live in cold climates.

Time — Perhaps the bee would mutate gradually, because of new diets.

Test #8: The Nomad With The Gold Rod

Cut the rod into 3 pieces: 1, 2 and 4 kg.

At the beginning, give the rider the 1-kg. piece. After the first km give him the 2-kg. piece, and take back the 1-kg. piece. At km 3, give him the 1-kg. piece (Rider now has 3 kg.). Follow this procedure for the rest of the journey.

Test #9: The Defective Vending Machine

Take candy bars from all the machines: 1 from the first machine, 2 from the second, 3 from the third, etc. Now weigh all of them; in the absence of a defective machine, the total weight should be 550 grams. If the machine reads 546 grams (4 grams less), then we know that machine no. 4, which provided 4 candy bars, is the defective machine.

Test #10, #11, #12:

The reader should run *XpertUS,* fill in the corresponding tables and compare results.

References

1. Miller, George: The Magic Number Seven; *The Psychological Review*, 63 (1956): 81-97.

2. Center for Defense Information: *Terrorism Project;* Nov. 30, 2001

3. Hamel, Gary and Prahalad, C.K.: *Competing for the Future;* Harvard Business School Press.

4. Bales, J.; *Vincennes:* APA Monitor, Dec. 1989: 10-11.

5. Fortune Magazine *Website:* 04/01/2002.

6. Roberts, Michel: *The Power of Strategic Thinking;* McGraw-Hill

7. *http://www.abovetopsecret.com/pages/area51.html*

8. Wallace, Graham: *The Art of Thought;* not available in print.

9. Osborne, Alex: *Applied Imagination;* Scribner; 1953.

10. Trompenaars, Fons and Hampden-Turner, Charles: *Riding The Waves Of Culture;* McGraw-Hill.

11. Internet site: *www.parc.xerox.com*

12. Blanchard, Ken; *The One Minute Manager;* McGraw Hill.

13. *Accounting Age;* The Daily Mirror; 14th July 1999.

14. De Bono, Edward; *Opportunities;* Penguin Books; 1984.

15. Wolford, Taylor & Beck: *The Conjunction Fallacy;* Memory & Cognition, 18 (1990): 48-53.

Index

Abu Dhabi, 68, 147
Afghanistan, 48, 60, 74, 207-209
Aim-Preset, 86, 91, 154, 217
Aircraft engines, 92
Alcatraz, 19
Alcohol, 47, 234, 242
Algorithmic, 103
Amoco, 82
Amway, 85
Apple, 15
Arab League, 143
Arabs, 54, 102
Area 51,
Armed Forces, 35
Arms, 24
Artificial intelligence, 42
Asians, 54
Assigning, 100, 109, 112, 116,
    124, 163, 184, 204
Astrologers, 32
Attitude, 44-45, 90, 177, 212
Automobile, 6, 16, 27, 46, 70, 90,
    99, 187
Automotive engines, 92
Aztecs, 79

Babbage, Charles, 18
Balance, 7, 64, 224, 226
Bank teller, 233, 241
Bengal tigers, 84

Betamax, 16
Bias, 4, 50, 116, 123
Bic Corporation, 10
Bid Evaluation, 35, 163-165, 167
Billboards, 26-27, 200
Bin Laden, Osama 97, 207-208
Biofuel, 80
Biological clock, 88
Blanchard, Ken 133
Bloody Sunday, 17
Bobsledding, 132
Botanist, 6
Brainstorming, 79, 157, 201, 211,
    213-216
British Airways, 80
Brother Company, 3, 72
Burger King, 93, 97, 153
Bush, George, 145, 208
Bush, George W., 3, 24, 47, 57,
    104, 152
Butter, 104

Candidate selection, 105-106,
    108-110, 153
Canon, 72, 78
Carnegie, Dale 3, 109
Carter, Jimmy, 63
Census, 36, 64-65
Challenger, 134
Cheetah, 128

Chevron, 82, 208

Chlorine, 89

Chrysler, 81, 130-131

Churchill, Winston, 18

Circular cultures, 97

Civilian, 34

Clinton, Bill, 48, 68, 101-102

Cognitive, 42, 80

Columbia, 17, 135

Common fallacy, 102

Communitarian, 56

Comparison, 41, 110, 116, 123-124, 165, 204, 217, 221

Compartmentalized, 62

Competition, 59, 62, 68-70, 72

Comprehension, 5, 44, 49

Compromising, 226

Conflict resolution, 25

Conjunction Rule, 241

Conoco, 82

Consensus, 8, 35, 126, 135-136

Consistency, 15

Consistent, 15, 105, 124, 163, 166, 170, 204-205, 217, 219, 221

Consolidation, 136, 164, 167, 205

Contracts, 48, 62, 141-143, 145, 147-148

Cool Runnings, 132

Cows, 81

Creative thinking, 69, 75-78, 86, 104-105, 175, 196

Creativity, 75, 82, 100, 104-105, 193, 213-215

Credibility, 85, 204, 227

Criteria selection, 99-100, 103, 110, 116, 153, 203

Criteria weighting, 111, 116, 181

Criteria weights, 111, 164, 166, 188

Cross-fertilization, 53, 77, 79-80, 82, 91, 101, 136

Cultural heritage, 56, 97

Cultural values, 57

Darwin, Charles, 7, 98

De Bono, Edward, 83, 232, 240

De Gaulle, Charles, 133

DEA, 85, 101

Death penalty, 7, 135, 144

Decision trees, 41

Delegating, 33, 133

Delta Force, 74

Demographics, 39, 59, 64-65, 84, 91

Desirable, 105, 110, 122-123, 153, 166, 183, 235

Dissect, 24, 123

Distribution technique, 41, 111-112, 152, 158, 235

Dow Jones, 36

Dowd, Maureen, 141

DNA, 14

Drucker, Peter, 3, 117

Dubai, 68-69, 144

Dumb dog, 240

Dupont, 78-79

Egypt, 129

Einstein, Albert, 95

Elf Aquitane, 81

Emirates Airline, 69

Encarta, 69

Encyclopedia Britannica, 69, 144

Enron, 73

ERP, 9

Euro, 66

Execution, 127-129

External factors, 59, 61, 63, 65, 67, 69, 71, 73

Exxon, 36

Eye-level, 29

Fast-food, 64, 93, 97, 153
Federal Express, 130
FedEx, 130
Feminist, 233, 241
Fina, 81
Fire-sale, 145
Fireworks, 66
Fishermen, 75
Focus groups, 35, 79
Forbes, Steve, 17
Force Field Analysis, 117
Ford, Harrison, 17
Ford Motor Company, 81
Forecasting, 40
Foreign markets, 92
Fortune 500, 32, 66-67
Fortune-tellers, 32
Fosbury flop, 83
Foyer, 240
Frame of Mind, 44, 51-52
Framework, 40
Fuzzy logic, 42

Gambling, 14, 37, 39
General Motors, 72, 81, 117
Geopolitics, 59, 67, 91, 121, 161
Gertsner, Lou, 80
Globalization, 56
Groupthink, 134-135
Gulf Air, 68-69, 144
Gut-feelings, 5, 10, 133

Harley Davidson, 63
Heuristics, 38
Home Depot, 80
Homebuyer, 107, 111, 238
Homicide bombers, 50
Honda, 92, 154
Human Resources, 102, 157, 161, 169, 171, 173, 175, 177-178

Humana Corp., 94
Hussein, Saddam, 145

Iacocca, Lee, 99
IBM, 15, 72, 80
Idealab, 16
Ignorance, 4, 52, 99
IKEA, 80
Imagination, 44, 53, 82
Implementation, 9, 31, 35, 127
Implementing, 7, 127-129, 131
Impossibility, 71-72
Inconsistencies, 204
India, 57
Individualistic, 56
Information gathering, 155
Information Technology, 8-9
Inherent limitations, 43-45, 47, 49, 51, 53, 55, 57, 59
Intelligence, 42, 72, 208
Interdependent, 25
Internet, 9, 16, 26, 73, 83, 85, 130, 188, 200, 218
Interpretations, 215
Interruptible, 106
Invisibility, 71
Iraq, 145
Islamic, 49
Israelis, 25-26, 104

Jaegermeister, 56, 84, 85
Jamaican, 132
Japan, 3, 46
Japanese, 3, 6, 36, 54
Judgment, 18, 41, 99, 110, 113, 116-117, 121, 133-134, 137, 140, 148, 153-156, 221
Judgment table, 154-155
JVC, 16, 131

Kaplan, 67

Kennedy, John F., 131

Killer bees, 87

Kissinger, Henry, 11

Kmart, 17

Knowledge, 5-6, 23, 26, 33, 43-44, 53-54, 70, 72, 82, 99, 147, 171-173, 175, 189, 211, 241

Kroc, Ray, 13

Kuwait, 64, 144

Lateral thinking, 83, 86, 231-232, 240

Leader, 3, 31, 136, 161, 164, 172, 208-209

Lebanon, 48

Lewinsky, Monica, 48

Libyan Airliner, 41, 71, 207

Limiting condition, 107

Linda's profession, 233, 241

Logic, 3, 42, 121, 133, 233

Lumberjack, 6

Malaysia, 56

Mao Tse-tung, 44

Margarine, 104

Market value, 145

Marketing strategists, 26

Martyrdom, 50

Maskelyne, xiv

Mathematical tools, 38, 40, 122

Mathematics, 39, 54, 124, 190, 231

Matrix Method, 114, 116, 124, 137, 156, 164

Maturity, 121, 133, 180

McDonald's, 13, 55

Memory, 5, 44, 54, 118

Mercedes Benz, 6

Metcalf, Jason, 48

Methodology, 38, 171, 235

Mexican economy, 68

Microsoft, 15, 62, 67, 69, 72, 144

Middle East, 25, 68, 104, 143

Military, 26, 59, 63-64, 80, 93, 128, 208

Miller, George, 43, 46

Mobil, 81

Monkey, 76, 88

NASA, 47, 89, 134-135

Need-to-have, 109

Negotiate, 27, 63, 143, 145-148, 208

Negotiations, 25, 141, 143-145, 147-148, 165, 223

Netscape, 67

New Zealand, 104

News Corp, 16

Nice-to-have, 109

Nigeria, 59, 88

Not-So-Identical Coins, 231, 239

Numerator, 26

Objective, 4, 45

Obligatory, 109-110, 122, 151, 154, 156, 166, 180-181, 183-184, 188, 192-193, 196, 200

Obsolescence, 96

Oil companies, 61-62, 82

Oman, 68

Operational research, 40

Opportunity seeking, 10, 11

Optimum, 4, 22, 25, 75, 84, 86, 103, 119, 123, 127, 134, 136, 170

Osborn, Alex, 82

Overconfidence, 34, 44, 52-53

Pairwise comparison, 110, 123-124, 217, 221

Pakistan, 60, 209

Palestinians, 25, 104

Pattern recognition, 36

Pepsi, 16, 93

Perishable, 95, 97, 106, 129

Persian Gulf, 34
Persistence, 128-132, 175
Pessimists, 104
Pharmaceutical stocks, 100-101
Pitt, Harvey, 135
Planning, 90
PMI Technique, 117
PointCast, 16
Policy changes, 59, 66, 195
Port of Los Angeles, 227
Postpone, 34
Potential, 11, 63, 91, 102, 134, 136,
    142, 144-146, 171, 175, 177, 180,
    184, 187, 190, 195, 238
Powell, Colin, 18, 148
Power of Reasoning, 231
Practitioners, 229
Prerequisites, 107-110, 117, 151, 153-
    154, 165-166, 176, 180-181, 183-
    184, 187-188, 195-196, 199-200
Princeton Review, 67
Probability, 14, 39-40, 143, 241
Problem-solving, 11, 175
Process of elimination, 41, 107
Proposals, 18, 146
Pros & Cons Method, 116
Pseudo-rational arguments, 4, 38

Qualitative, 5, 21-22, 111, 122
Quantitative, 5, 21, 42, 73, 122, 158,
    204
Quarterbacks, 23-24
Queen's English, 37
Quick-fix, 25
Quixtar, 85

Radon gas, 88
Random-sampling, 122
Rank-Frequency Technique, 139

Ranking, 11, 41, 46, 75, 109-113, 115,
    117-119, 122, 124-125, 136-139,
    146, 156, 164, 167, 174, 181, 203-
    204, 220
Rational, 23, 27, 116, 121
Rationalize, 23, 27
Reagan, Ronald, 32
Real Estate, 102, 161, 183, 185
Reasoning, 5-6, 42, 44, 53-54, 121,
    133, 231, 242
Recruiting, 23, 35, 102, 138, 161
Refineries, 61-62
Regulatory, 10, 59, 66, 121
Reliability, 124-125, 130, 187, 201,
    204, 217-219, 221
Reliability index, 124
Remington, 63
Retail sales, 29
Return on investment, 195
Revenue, 24, 45, 61, 64, 79, 88, 92,
    102, 106, 152, 173, 215
Right-handed, 29
Rogers, Will, 9
Roosevelt, Theodore, 10-11, 93
Root cause analysis, 40

Saudi Royal Plane, 57
Saxon, John, 130
Scaling Technique, 41, 111, 124
Schwarzenegger, Arnold,
Seals, 82, 134
Sears, 28
Segregation, 109, 111, 196, 200
Sensitivity studies, 125, 205
Sequential cultures, 97
Serbia, 64
Service Merchandise, 83
Shell Oil Co., 82, 90
Sho Yano, xv
Smart, Barry, 157, 170

Smith Corona, 72
Smith, Fred, 130
Soccer, 53, 84
Sony, 16
South America, 141-142
Southwest Airlines, 37, 72
Soviet Empire, 60
Sri Lanka, 105
Standard Oil, 93
Statistical, 241
Strategic planning, 91, 175
Strategic thinking, 81, 91, 148
Subjective, 4-5, 40-41, 73, 110, 117, 171, 203-204, 221
Sub-optimal, 44, 103, 128, 204
Success triangle, 128-129
Suicide, 26, 48, 50
Superstition, 36
Sydney Harbor Bridge, 50
Syria, 129

Tactical, 91-93, 152
Tank Farms, 61
Tapestry, 7
Team Decisions, 134
Telemarketing, 26, 200
Tenacious, 128, 130-132
Territory, 3, 71, 215
Terrorism, 24, 49, 60, 67
Texaco, 81
Thatcher, Margaret, 31, 38
Timing, 95, 97, 101-102, 128-129, 131, 161
Tires, 27, 73, 88
Tools, 10, 25, 31, 33, 35, 37-41, 75, 122, 134
Top-skewed scenario, 125, 157
Total-Point Technique, 138-139
Toxic lead, 16
Toyota, 72

Training, 10, 112, 134, 162, 169-170, 175-176, 185, 205, 217
Traits, 5, 59, 175
Transparency, 8, 123, 163, 169, 204
Trompenaars, Frans, 97

U.S. Congress, 35, 134, 208
U.S. Constitution, 8
U.S. Senate, 8, 135
Uncertainty, 113, 189
Unique, 5, 22, 78, 114
Urgent, 129, 175, 237

Vaccines, 88
Valenti, Jack, 88
Venezuela, 55
VHS, 16, 88
Vincennes, 34
Virtues, 133, 201, 217, 219, 221
Vision, 44, 53, 79-80, 83, 104, 132
Volvo, 6

Wallace, Graham, 75
Wal-Mart, 17, 37, 65, 79, 84
Wayne, John, 65
Weinberger, Caspar, 85
White House, 48, 50, 57, 72, 145
Windows, 62
Wisdom, 79, 84, 121, 133, 143
Wording Effect, 49

Xerox, 15, 72, 79, 130

Yale University, 130, 134
Yin-yang, 7
Yom Kippur War, 95, 129
Young, Cliff, 19

The "Aim-Preset"™ Technique

This stands for: *Accept, Isolate, Modify, Problem, Replace, External, Sacrifice, Environment, and Time.* When you go through these steps, you will explore all possible solutions.

A — Can I simply *accept* the problem and live with it?

I — Can I *isolate* the product/system from the harmful influence?

M — Can I *modify* the product or the system?

P — Is it possible that the solution might be in the *problem*?

R — Can I degrade the product and/or *replace* it?

E — Can I eliminate or mitigate the *external* cause?

S — Can I use direct or indirect *sacrificial* techniques?

E — Can I change the *environment* in which the problem thrives?

T — Will the passage of *time* resolve the problem?

$100.00
Gift Certificate

This offer is only for use of the XpertUS decision-maker. It has no cash value. Complete this certificate or a copy, and mail it with the *original purchase receipt*. Shanmar Publishing will send you the access code to use XpertUS, with instructions.

If you do not have email access, you *must* include a self-addressed, stamped envelope.

Name: _____

Address: _____

Email address: _____

Phone No: _____; Fax No: _____

For mailing address visit www.xpertus.com

- Requests for access code must be submitted within 90 days of purchase of book
- Offer valid for personal use only.

Know the author . . .

D<small>R</small>. W<small>IRASINGHE</small>, a native of Sri Lanka, was educated in the U.K.

As an Oil & Gas industry specialist and a University Professor, Wirasinghe has published papers on topics relating to Management, Engineering, and Economics.

He has over 25 years of experience in Optimization, Creative Thinking, Opportunity Seeking, Decision-Making, and Strategic Planning for Shell Oil Co., Petroleos de Venezuela, Abu Dhabi National Oil Co., Williams, and Enron.

Fluent in several languages, and familiar with a variety of cultures and values that govern religious, social and business conduct in many countries, Dr. Wirasinghe has conducted consulting assignments for many foreign clients. Several of his consulting projects have included negotiations on behalf of international clients.

He is an entertaining speaker with a global outlook and a passion for decision-making. He brings a wealth of real-life experience, and has helped many organizations add value to their human assets.

Dr. Wirasinghe is a guest lecturer at several MBA programs, and has also appeared on radio talk shows. He has been featured in several prestigious magazines, including the *Continental*, a publication of Continental Airlines.

In *The Art of Making Decisions—Expanding Common Sense and Experience*, he unravels the myth and the math of decision-making, and offers a simple seven-step process for optimum decision-making.

Dr. Wirasinghe has also developed a software package, the *XpertUS* multi-dimensional decision-maker.

This book, along with the *XpertUS* software and his training courses, provides a unique set of tools to enhance decision-making.

Feel free to contact Dr. Wirasinghe via e-mail: author@XpertUS.com

—⋙〢⋘—

TRAINING COURSES

Shanmar Inc. offers a comprehensive series of seminars in decision-making, creative thinking, and negotiations.